Solutions and Tests

for

Exploring Creation

with

Marine
Biology

by Sherri Seligson

Solutions and Tests for Exploring Creation with Marine Biology

Published by
Apologia Educational Ministries, Inc.
1106 Meridian Plaza, Suite 220
Anderson, IN 46016
www.apologia.com

Manufactured in the United States of America
Second Printing 2006

ISBN: 1-932012-59-1

Printed by The C.J. Krehbiel Company, Cincinnati, OH

Cover photos: Dolphins (© Bill Boyce/oceanwideimages.com), Rocky-Bottom Subtidal Community (© Gary Bell/oceanwideimages.com), Whale Breaching (© Mark Simmons/oceanwideimages.com)

Cover design by Kim Williams

Exploring Creation with Marine Biology
Solutions and Tests

TABLE OF CONTENTS

Tests

Solutions to the Tests

Quarterly Tests and Solutions

Solutions to the Quarterly Tests

TEACHER'S NOTES
Exploring Creation with Marine Biology

Thank you for choosing *Exploring Creation with Marine Biology*. We designed this course to meet the needs of the homeschooling parent. We are very sensitive to the fact that most homeschooling parents do not know marine biology very well, if at all. As a result, they consider it nearly impossible to teach to their children. This course has several features that make it ideal for such a parent:

1. The course is written in a conversational style. Unlike many authors, Mrs. Seligson does not get wrapped up in the desire to write formally. As a result, the text is easy to read, and the student feels more like he or she is *learning*, not just reading.

2. The course is completely self-contained. Each module in the student text includes the text of the lesson, experiments to perform, and questions to answer. This book contains the solutions to the study guide questions, tests, and solutions to the tests.

3. The experiments use a lot of materials that are readily available at either the grocery or the hardware store. If you wish to perform every experiment contained in the course, however, you will need to purchase equipment we make available for this course. A list of the equipment is presented in the "Student Notes" section of the student text.

4. Most importantly, this course is Christ-centered. In every way possible, we try to make the science of marine biology glorify God. One of the most important things you and your student should get out of this course is a deeper appreciation for the wonder of God's creation!

Pedagogy of the Text

There are two types of exercises the student is expected to complete: "On Your Own" questions and study guide questions.

- The "On Your Own" questions should be answered as the student reads the text. The act of answering these questions will cement in the student's mind the concepts he or she is trying to learn. The answers to these questions are included as a part of the student text. The student should feel free to use those answers to check his or her work.

- The study guide questions help the student review what has been covered in a module and should be answered after the student completes the module. They will help the student recall the important concepts from the reading. As your student's teacher, you can decide whether or not your student can look at the answers to these questions. They are located in this book.

In addition to the questions discussed above, there is also a test for each module. You have our permission to copy the tests out of this book if you would prefer to do that instead of administering the tests directly out of this book. **We strongly recommend that you administer each test once the student has completed the module and all the associated exercises. The student should be allowed to have only pencil and paper while taking the test.**

Any information the student must memorize is centered in the text and put in boldface type. Any boldface words (centered or not) are terms with which the student must be familiar. In addition, all definitions presented in the text need to be memorized.

You will notice that every answer contains an underlined section. That is the actual answer to the question. The rest is simply an explanation of how to get the answer. For questions that require a sentence or paragraph as an answer, the student need not have *exactly* what is given in this book. The basic message of his or her answer, however, has to be the same as the basic message of the answer given in this book.

Experiments

The experiments in this course are designed to be done as the student is reading the text. We recommend that your student keep a notebook of these experiments. The details of how to perform the experiments and how to keep a laboratory notebook are discussed in the "Student Notes" section of the student text.

Grading

Grading your student is an important part of this course. We recommend that you *correct* the study guide questions, but we do not recommend that you include the student's score in his or her grade. Instead, we recommend that the student's grade be composed solely of test grades and laboratory notebook grades. Here is what we suggest you do:

1. Give the student a grade for each lab that is done. This grade should not reflect the accuracy of the student's results. Rather, it should reflect how well the student followed directions and how well he or she wrote up the lab in his or her lab notebook.

2. Give the student a grade for each test. In the test solutions, you will see a point value assigned to each problem. If your student answered the question correctly, he or she should receive the number of points listed. If your student got a portion of the answer correct, he or she should receive a portion of those points. Your student's percentage grade, then, can be calculated as follows:

$$\text{Student's Grade} = \frac{\text{\# of points received}}{\text{\# of points possible}} \times 100$$

The number of possible points for each test is listed at the bottom of the solutions.

3. The student's overall grade in the course should be weighted as follows: 35% lab grade and 65% test grade. If you really feel that you must include the study guides in the student's total grade, make the labs worth 35%, the tests worth 55%, and the study guides worth 10%. A straight 90/80/70/60 scale should be used to calculate the student's letter grade. This is typical for most schools. If you have your own grading system, please feel free to use it. This grading system is only a suggestion.

SOLUTIONS TO THE STUDY GUIDE FOR MODULE #1

1. a. Oceanic crust – The portion of the earth's crust that primarily contains basalt, is relatively dense, and is about 5 kilometers thick

b. Continental crust – The portion of the earth's crust that primarily contains granite, is less dense than oceanic crust, and is 20 to 50 kilometers thick

c. Plate tectonics – A process involving the movement of large plates on the earth's mantle

d. Mid-ocean ridge – A continuous chain of underwater volcanic mountains encompassing the earth

e. Seafloor spreading – The process that creates new sea floor as an area moves away from the mid-ocean ridges

f. Subduction – The downward movement of one plate into the earth's mantle when two plates collide

g. Continental shelf – The gently sloped, shallow section of the edge of a continent, extending from the shore to the point where the slope gets steeper

h. Continental slope – The steeper section of a continental edge, extending seaward from the continental shelf

i. Continental rise – The gently sloping area at the base of the continental slope

j. Specific heat – The amount of energy required to raise the temperature of one gram of a substance by $1.00\,^\circ$ C

k. Salinity – The total amount of salt dissolved in a solvent

l. Coriolis effect – The way in which the rotation of the earth bends the path of winds and resulting sea currents

m. Gyres – Large, mostly circular systems of surface currents driven by the wind

n. Spring tide – A time of largest tidal range due to the gravitational pull of the aligned sun and moon (during full moon and new moon)

o. Neap tide – A time of smallest tidal range due to the moon and sun being located at right angles to each other (during quarter moons)

2. The four large ocean basins of the world in order of increasing size are the Arctic Ocean, the Indian Ocean, the Atlantic Ocean, and the Pacific Ocean.

3. The differences between these types of crust are in the chemical and physical composition of the rocks. Whether or not they are covered by water is irrelevant. Oceanic crust contains basalt and is denser and thinner than continental crust, which contains granite, is less dense, and is thicker.

4.   Since earthquakes are often caused when plates move relative to one another, <u>two plates are probably moving relative to one another underneath that location</u>.

5.   Subduction tends to form trenches. Thus, <u>subduction must be occurring in the Pacific Ocean</u>.

6.   New oceanic crust is formed at the ocean ridges, where plates are moving apart. The Altantic Ocean has the large mid-ocean ridge, so <u>oceanic crust formation mostly occurs in the Atlantic Ocean</u>. Oceanic crust is destroyed at the trenches, where subduction occurs. Problem #5 tells you that this occurs in the Pacific Ocean, so <u>oceanic crust destruction occurs mostly in the Pacific Ocean</u>.

7.   Most marine life is found in the areas of the <u>continental shelf</u>. This relatively shallow part of the sea is where more sunlight can penetrate and therefore more producers can survive. The abundance of producers provides more opportunity for animal life to thrive as well.

8.   The major property of water that keeps its molecules held together is <u>hydrogen bonding</u>.

9.   <u>Water has a high specific heat</u>, so despite drastic air temperature changes, the water's temperature does not change very quickly.

10. <u>Evaporation will result in greater salinity of the water left behind. This water will then become denser and could begin to sink to a lower level in the ocean. A drop in temperature will do the same thing, because colder water is denser than warmer water</u>.

11. The ocean is blue because <u>the wavelengths of blue light can penetrate much deeper than those of other colors. Also, the blue sky reflects off the surface of the ocean</u>, enhancing the blue color.

12. Since the grouper lived at the bottom of the ocean, <u>its body was acclimated to the extra pressure of water above its habitat. When it was brought to the surface very quickly, the gases in its body experienced much less pressure so they expanded, resulting in its bloated look, and caused it to die</u>.

13. Winds do not move in a straight line because of the <u>Coriolis effect</u>. The rotation of the earth bends the path of the winds.

14. <u>The gyres would flow in the opposite directions</u>, because the winds would be bent in the opposite directions. Thus, the Northern Hemisphere gyres would be counterclockwise, while the Southern Hemisphere gyres would be clockwise.

15. <u>They move in a circular motion down under the water and back up to their original position</u>. Only energy is transferred along the waves.

16. <u>During the full moon and the new moon</u> is when the tidal ranges are their largest because this is when the moon is aligned with the sun and their gravitational attractions work together.

17. <u>The surface layer is a well-mixed layer exposed to wind and currents and is generally warmer in temperature. The deep layer is uniformly cold and much thicker than the surface layer. The thermocline separates them and is a transitional zone between them</u>.

SOLUTIONS TO THE STUDY GUIDE FOR MODULE #2

1. a. Metabolism – The process by which a living organism takes energy from its surroundings and uses it to sustain itself, develop and grow

b. Photosynthesis – The process by which an organism uses the energy from the sun to produce its own food

c. Autotrophs – Organisms that are able to produce their own food

d. Heterotrophs – Organisms that cannot make their own food and must obtain it from other organisms

e. Respiration – The process by which food is converted into useable energy for life functions

f. Homeostasis – The tendency of living organisms to control or regulate changes in their internal environment

g. Diffusion – The movement of molecules from an area of high concentration to an area of low concentration

h. Osmosis – The diffusion of water across a selectively permeable membrane

i. Osmoconformer – An organism that allows its internal concentration of salts to change in order to match the external concentration of salts in the surrounding water

j. Osmoregulator – An organism that regulates its internal concentration of salts

k. Poikilotherm – An organism whose body temperature changes with its surrounding environment

l. Ectotherm – An organism whose body temperature is controlled by its surrounding environment

m. Homeotherm – An animal that maintains a controlled internal body temperature using its own heating and cooling mechanisms

n. Endotherm – An animal whose internal body temperature is a result of internal sources of heat

o. Asexual reproduction – Reproduction accomplished by a single organism

p. Sexual reproduction – Reproduction that involves the union of gametes from two organisms: a male and a female

q. Binomial nomenclature – Identifying an organism by its genus and species name

2. The four main groups of molecules involved in metabolism are carbohydrates, proteins, lipids, and nucleic acids.

3. At night there would be no oxygen produced because there would be no photosynthesis (of which oxygen is a byproduct). Therefore the oxygen levels would be lower at night than in the day.

4. No, heterotrophs need to feed on the stored excess material produced by photosynthesizing autotrophs. If there is little sunlight, there will be little excess material upon which heterotrophs can feed.

5. No, because both of these groups contain organisms with these features. Eukaryotic cells have membrane-bound organelles and prokaryotic cells do not.

6. The two organisms in the population would be most similar since, by definition, a population is when multiple organisms of the same species coexist together. An ecosystem contains many different species.

7. The concentration of sugar on the outside of the strawberry cells is higher than the dissolved solids inside the cells. As a result, water will travel via osmosis to the outside of the cells.

8. The body fluids of the osmoconformer would change, because it must adjust the concentration of dissolved substances in its body fluids to match its environment. As a result, the concentration of dissolved substances in its body fluids would increase.

9. Not really. These organisms' body temperatures change with their environments, so they could have warm blood if their environment was warm.

10. Yes. The only way you can regulate your body's temperature is to have an internal source of heat.

11. No. A shark is a poikilotherm, because the temperature of its environment affects its body temperature. However, it is also an endotherm, because its muscles heat its body.

12. The plant grown from the cutting would be more like the nursery plant, because the asexual reproduction would produce an exact genetic copy.

13. The cell with 24 chromosomes is the diploid cell. Diploid cells have chromosomes that come in pairs. Haploid cells have one chromosome from each of those pairs; thus, they have half as many chromosomes as diploid cells. Since cells can be only diploid or haploid, the cell with the most chromosomes is the diploid cell.

14. The cell with 12 chromosomes came from germ tissue, because germ tissue produces gametes, which are haploid.

15. Yes, common names for creatures are as varied as the people that describe them. An organism's genus and species names, however, are unique to it.

SOLUTIONS TO THE STUDY GUIDE FOR MODULE #3

1. a. <u>Bacteria</u> – Prokaryotic, single-celled, microscopic organisms

b. <u>Decomposers</u> – Organisms that break down dead organic matter into smaller molecules

c. <u>Chemosynthesis</u> – A process that derives energy from specific chemical compounds

d. <u>Phytoplankton</u> – Microscopic photosynthetic organisms that drift in the water

e. <u>Zooplankton</u> – Tiny floating organisms that are either small animals or protozoa

f. <u>Thallus</u> – The complete body of an alga, not differentiated into true leaves, stems, or roots

g. <u>Diploid</u> – A cell that contains two similar sets of chromosomes

h. <u>Haploid</u> – A cell that contains half the normal number of chromosomes

i. <u>Alternation of generations</u> – A life cycle that alternates between a sexual stage (gametophyte) and an asexual stage (sporophyte)

j. <u>Symbiosis</u> – A close relationship between two species where at least one benefits

k. <u>Lichen</u> – An organism that results from the symbiosis between a fungus and an alga

2. Heterotrophic bacteria are known as <u>decomposers</u>.

3. Even though these organisms look like algae, <u>they are prokaryotic</u>, which makes them more like bacteria.

4. <u>Cyanobacteria convert atmospheric nitrogen into a form of nitrogen that can be used by other creatures in Creation.</u>

5. Photosynthetic diatoms are considered to be the greatest producers of <u>oxygen</u> on the planet. Without their contribution to the oxygen supply, many life forms, including humans, could not survive.

6. <u>Diatoms can asexually reproduce by splitting their frustules; they can asexually reproduce by shedding their frustules and forming an auxospore; and they can sexually reproduce by forming gametes that make an auxospore after fertilization.</u>

7. <u>When diatoms split their frustules</u>, one of the offspring will be smaller than the parent.

8. <u>Dinoflagellates have two flagella.</u> One trails behind the body, and the other is wrapped around the body's middle.

9. Since the water is red, the area is most likely experiencing a bloom of unicellular algae. <u>You should not eat the fish, because some microorganisms that bloom can release toxins that harm you.</u> If you eat the fish, you might be eating those toxins.

10. They are swimming in their nutrient supply, so the needed nutrients and unnecessary waste products can diffuse through their cell membranes. They therefore do not need any specialized structures to accomplish this.

11. As foraminiferans die, large deposits of their shells accumulate on the ocean floor. Scientists have found some of these deposits on land, which leads them to believe these areas were once underwater.

12. A thallus can have blades, pneumatocysts, a stipe, and a holdfast.

13. They use a substance from brown algae, called algin, that works as an emulsifying agent that helps the oil and vinegar to stay mixed together.

14. A diploid gametophyte generation (2n) will result. If the life cycle is alternation of generations, then the sporophyte generation will always give rise to the gametophyte generation, and vice versa. Also, the generations switch between diploid (2n) and haploid (1n). Thus, if the current generation is haploid (1n), the next generation will have to be diploid (2n).

15. If the gametophyte generation is haploid, its cells have only half the chromosomes of the diploid cell. Gametes *must* also be haploid, as they add their DNA during fertilization to make a diploid cell. Thus, this haploid alga must make haploid cells. The only way this can happen is through mitosis, as mitosis produces daughter cells that have the same number of chromosomes as the parent cell. If a haploid parent cell were to undergo meiosis, the daughter cells would have only ¼ of the diploid DNA, as meiosis produces daughter cells with half the DNA as the parent cell.

16. They are both decomposers.

17. In a lichen, the fungus provides support for the alga, and the alga provides food produced from photosynthesis.

18. The seagrasses are the one group of true marine plants because they can spend their entire lives under the sea.

19. Seagrass sexual reproduction is much like the sexual reproduction in land plants. The seagrasses produce male gametes, called pollen, that float in the currents. If pollen lands on the flower of another seagrass of the same species, fertilization occurs, producing a seed.

20. They produce large prop roots that trap sediments. The trapped sediment can build up, creating more land area.

SOLUTIONS TO THE STUDY GUIDE FOR MODULE #4

1. a. <u>Osculum</u> – A large opening on a sponge through which filtered water is expelled

b. <u>Amoebocytes</u> – Cells within a sponge that produce its skeletal structure, perform digestion, and repair cell damage

c. <u>Gemmule</u> – A group of cells surrounded by a shell made of spicules

d. <u>Metamorphosis</u> – A complete morphological change from larval to adult form

e. <u>Spherical symmetry</u> – A body form in which any cut through the organism's center results in identical halves

f. <u>Radial symmetry</u> – A body form in which any longitudinal cut through the organism's central axis results in identical halves

g. <u>Bilateral symmetry</u> – A body form in which only one longitudinal cut through the organism's center results in identical halves

h. <u>Polyp</u> – An attached cnidarian stage, appearing sac-like or barrel-like

i. <u>Medusa</u> – A free-swimming cnidarian stage, appearing bell-like or umbrella-like

j. <u>Mesoglea</u> – A jelly-like substance between the inner layer and outer layer of cells in a cnidarian

k. <u>Dorsal</u> – Referring to the top (or back) surface of an animal

l. <u>Ventral</u> – Referring to the bottom (or belly) surface of an animal

m. <u>Mutualism</u> – A relationship between two or more organisms of different species where both benefit from the association

n. <u>Commensalism</u> – A relationship between two or more organisms of different species where one benefits and the other is neither harmed nor benefited

o. <u>Parasitism</u> – A relationship between two or more organisms of different species where one benefits and the other is harmed

p. <u>Coelom</u> – A body cavity within organisms containing specialized tissue

q. <u>Gills</u> – Extensions of the body containing thin-walled blood vessels that allow for easy absorption of oxygen from the outside surface

2. <u>Most large species of sponges contain spicules for support. Since spicules are very sharp and abrasive, they would be of no use to people wanting to wash dishes or their cars.</u>

3. <u>The larvae can settle in other areas of the ocean to avoid over-populating one place.</u>

4. Collar cells move water through the sponge by beating their flagella back and forth. They also trap and collect food.

5. Amoebocytes secrete the spicules and spongin, transport and digest food, expel wastes, produce gametes, and repair damaged portions of the sponge.

6. Medusa and polyp are the two body forms of cnidarians. A medusa, with its tentacles dangling downward, is similar to an upside-down polyp. In addition, medusae are much more mobile than polyps.

7. A cnidarian's gastrovascular cavity has only one opening. A true gut has two.

8. A nematocyst is a stinging structure on a cnidarian's tentacle that discharges chemicals to paralyze prey or ward off predators.

9. Planula larvae are the result of sexual reproduction (see Figure 4.7).

10. Polyps reproduce by budding.

11. A Portuguese man-o-war is a *colony* of specialized polyps with different responsibilities. One polyp forms a gas-filled float that is sometimes mistaken for the bell of a jellyfish even though it does not undulate. Other polyps form the tentacles for stinging and capturing prey.

12. Jellyfish cannot swim strongly enough to avoid the motion of the currents. Thus, they drift with the current. Plankton are defined as organisms that drift with the current.

13. Hydrozoa: hydra, man-o-war
Scyphozoa: large jellyfish
Anthozoa: coral, sea fans, sea plumes, sea pens, sea anemones

14. Coral polyps secrete a hard calcium carbonate wall around their bodies, building on top of old skeletons of previous coral polyps to create a coral reef.

15. Zooxanthellae are dinoflagellates. They have a symbiotic relationship with coral polyps, providing the polyps with carbon-containing compounds, including food.

16. Their shape allows them to be active, receiving stimuli that need to be processed.

17. They are parasites, living in the intestines of their host. Since the intestine is where digested food is absorbed by the host's body, the tapeworm can absorb the nutrients into its body as well.

18. Fish are potential hosts of nematodes (roundworms). If the fish is not prepared properly, humans can become infected with this parasite by eating an infested host.

19. Its coelom is filled with fluid that helps support the body's structure. When the body's muscles contract in sequence against the pressure of the fluid-filled coelom, it gives the organism crawling ability.

20. <u>Gills contain thin-walled blood vessels that can directly absorb oxygen from the water.</u> This is important to creatures whose body walls are not thin, because the thicker the body wall, the harder it is for the organism's tissues to absorb oxygen directly.

21. <u>A suspension feeder is an organism that obtains its food from material suspended in the water.</u> A lophophorate is an example of a suspension feeder.

22. <u>Lamp shells have lophophores, since they are lophophorates. Clams do not. The shells on a clam are on the left and right sides of the clam's body, while the shells of a lamp shell are on the dorsal and ventral side of the lamp shell's body.</u>

SOLUTIONS TO THE STUDY GUIDE FOR MODULE #5

1. a. <u>Mantle</u> – A sheath of tissue surrounding the organs of a mollusk, producing the mollusk's shell and performing respiration

b. <u>Radula</u> – An organ covered with hundreds of small teeth used for scraping food into the mouths of mollusks

c. <u>Chitin</u> – A derivative of carbohydrates that provides both flexibility and support

d. <u>Open circulatory system</u> – A circulatory system in which blood flows out of the blood vessels and into body cavities, where it comes in direct contact with cells

e. <u>Closed circulatory system</u> – A circulatory system in which the blood always remains in vessels

f. <u>Molting</u> – The process of shedding an exoskeleton and replacing it with a new one

g. <u>Cephalothorax</u> – The anterior part of an arthropod body, consisting of a head and other body segments fused together

h. <u>Carapace</u> – An armored shield that covers the anterior portion of crustaceans

i. <u>Water vascular system</u> – A network of water-filled canals in echinoderms, used for locomotion and feeding

j. <u>Ambulacral groove</u> – A channel along the oral surface of echinoderms through which the tube feet protrude

k. <u>Notochord</u> – A flexible supportive rod that runs the length of the body of the chordates

l. <u>Dorsal nerve cord</u> – A long bundle of nerve cells located along the dorsal part of an organism's body

2. They both have a <u>mantle</u> enclosing their vital organs and performing respiration. They both also have a <u>radula</u> for scraping away bits of food.

3. a. The student need name only one: <u>snail, abalone, limpet</u>.
   b. The student need name only one: <u>clam, oyster, scallop</u>.
   c. The student need name only one: <u>octopus, squid, cuttlefish</u>.

4. The fact that its shell is made of two hinged halves pretty much tells you that it is in <u>class Bivalvia</u>.

5. Remember, <u>class Gastropoda</u> means the class of "stomach-foot" organisms.

6. Because they have no outer shell, <u>cephalopods can quickly contract their muscular mantle, expelling a jet of water out of their bodies and propelling them in the water</u>.

7. It has an <u>open circulatory system</u>. In a closed circulatory system, the blood stays in vessels and does not normally have direct contact with the tissues.

8. Most mollusks are hermaphroditic and thus are both male and female at the same time.

9. a. umbo b. muscle c. mouth d. foot e. gonad f. gut g. heart h. muscle i. anus
   j. siphons k. gills l. mantle

10. Because an arthropod has a hard exoskeleton, it cannot grow larger because the exoskeleton cannot stretch. Instead, the animal must molt. During the time it forms a new exoskeleton, the unprotected animal is more at risk of an attack from predators.

11. Crustaceans have an exoskeleton, gills, special appendages for swimming, and two pairs of antennae.

12. Their hard exoskeleton keeps moisture from escaping the body cavity, thus allowing the gills to stay moist.

13. The males transfer sperm directly to the females, who will store it to fertilize many batches of eggs.

14. Pentamerous symmetry is a type of radial symmetry based on five radiating parts.

15. The starfish ate the clam by penetrating the opening between its valves with the starfish's everted stomach. It can use its tube feet to gain a good grip on the clam and find even the tiniest opening between the valves in which to insert its stomach for digestion *before* it eats the clam.

16. Like all echinoderms, brittle stars have the ability to regenerate portions of their bodies. By detaching its arm, the brittle star was able to avoid getting eaten. It can easily grow a replacement.

17. The gametes are usually released during a short season of the year. Also, individuals of the same species will release their gametes when gametes of a like species are in the water. Each individual will release an enormous quantity of gametes, too.

18. a. water vascular system b. tube feet c. ampullae d. madreporite
    e. ambulacral grooves f. mouth

19. They have a leather-like "tunic" covering for support.

20. All chordates have a notochord and a dorsal nerve cord during at least one stage of their lives.

21. It could be a sea squirt. These creatures look a lot like sponges, but since they have a notochord in their larval form, they are not sponges.

22. The atrial cavity collects the water that the lancelet takes in for filtering and sends it out the body through the atriopore.

SOLUTIONS TO THE STUDY GUIDE FOR MODULE #6

1.a. <u>Anadromous</u> – A life cycle in which creatures are hatched in fresh water, migrate to salt water when adults, and return to fresh water in order to reproduce

b. <u>Demersal</u> – Fishes that live on the bottom of the ocean

c. <u>Chromatophores</u> – Surface pigment cells that expand and contract to produce various colors

d. <u>Myomeres</u> – Bands of muscle along the sides of fishes used for locomotion

e. <u>Gill rakers</u> – Projections along the inner surface of fishes' gills used for filter-feeding

f. <u>Migration</u> – The regular movement of an organism from one location to another

g. <u>Catadromous</u> – Referring to fishes that migrate from fresh water to reproduce in the ocean

h. <u>Hermaphroditism</u> – A situation in which an animal has the reproductive organs of both sexes

i. <u>Oviparous</u> – A type of development in which eggs are hatched outside a female's body

j. <u>Ovoviviparous</u> – A type of development in which eggs are hatched inside the female's body

k. <u>Viviparous</u> – A type of development in which the young obtain their nutrients directly from the mother and are birthed live

2. <u>An endoskeleton grows with the organism, so there is no need to molt.</u> During molting, creatures with exoskeletons have little protection and are, as a result, at great risk.

3. It is most likely in class <u>Agnatha</u>.

4. <u>Hagfishes occasionally will tie their eel-like bodies into a sliding knot in order to clean the excess slime from their bodies and to give them leverage when tearing apart food.</u>

5. <u>A lamprey begins its life in fresh water rivers and streams where it hatches out of its egg. It then eventually swims out to the ocean, where it will most commonly parasitze bony fishes while an adult. It will then travel back to fresh water rivers and streams to reproduce.</u>

6. This is a <u>bony fish</u>. Only true bone has osteocytes and osteoblasts.

7. <u>Sharks have rough, sandpaper-like skin due to tiny scales called denticles, which are made of the same material as that of teeth.</u>

8. a. <u>nare</u> b. <u>eye</u> c. <u>spiracle</u> d. <u>lateral line</u> e. <u>dorsal fins</u> f. <u>caudal fin</u> g. <u>anal fin</u> h. <u>pelvic fins</u> i. <u>pectoral fins</u> j. <u>gill slits</u> k. <u>mouth</u>

9. <u>Different sharks have very different tooth shapes.</u> You can often identify a shark just from its tooth.

10. <u>The largest sharks are filter feeders and do not eat anything larger than plankton.</u>

11. The plates are good for <u>crushing hard substances such as the shells of mollusks and crustaceans</u>.

12. It is a <u>skate</u>. The wing-like pectoral fins means it is not a shark, and rays have thin, whip-like tails.

13. <u>An operculum closes while water is let into the gills via the bony fish's mouth. This keeps water from flowing back in over the gills from the rear.</u> This results in a more efficient one-way flow of water.

14. <u>Sharks have a large, oily liver that aids in buoyancy. They also have large, fleshy pectoral fins that provide lift in the water column. Bony fishes have a balloon-like swim bladder in which the amounts of gas can be regulated.</u>

15. <u>A flounder is flattened laterally (from side to side), while a skate or ray is flattened dorsally (top to bottom).</u> One of the flounder's eyes travels over to the side facing up during its development as a young fish.

16. It is a <u>slow-moving reef-swimmer</u>. Fast-moving predators are tapered, while ray-like or flat fish are demersal. Eel-like fish live in the crevices of rocks and coral.

17. A <u>cleaner fish</u> would benefit from other fish knowing it is available to clean them. Also, <u>poisonous fishes</u> would benefit from making others aware of their dangerous protective ability.

18. <u>In filter fish, gill rakers catch the plankton that the fish eats. In other fish, they keep bits of food from getting into the gill slits.</u>

19. a. <u>heart</u> b. <u>liver</u> c. <u>kidney</u> d. <u>spleen</u> e. <u>rectum</u> f. <u>spiral intestine</u> g. <u>pancreas</u> h. <u>stomach</u>

20. Fishes have a <u>countercurrent system of flow over their gills</u> so that the oxygen levels in the water have a higher likelihood of being greater than that of the blood.

21. They have a <u>lateral line</u> along their bodies that is sensitive to vibrations and pressure changes in the water.

22. Sharks have <u>ampullae of Lorenzini</u> that can detect tiny electrical fields in the water.

23. <u>The one with the larger olfactory lobes</u> most likely came from the fish. Fish have a strong sense of smell that requires large olfactory lobes in the brain.

24. Fishes may school for the <u>protection</u> a group would provide. Others may school to help <u>round up prey while feeding</u>.

25. The resulting offspring will have a <u>more diverse genetic makeup</u> if the fish reproduces with another individual.

26. It is most likely <u>oviparous</u>. Since the eggs of oviparous fish are not protected, they lay thousands of eggs so that at least a few will hatch.

SOLUTIONS TO THE STUDY GUIDE FOR MODULE #7

1. a. <u>Adaptation</u> – An expression of a helpful trait coming directly from the genetic information already possessed by at least some individuals in a genetically diverse population

b. <u>Baleen</u> – Rows of comb-like horny plates that project from the upper jaws of filter-feeding whales

c. <u>Echolocation</u> – A method of analyzing sound waves to locate objects in the water column

d. <u>Behavior</u> – An activity an organism would do in its natural habitat

e. <u>Delayed implantation</u> – A delay in implantation of an embryo into the uterus allowing for the proper timing of birth

2. Sea turtles have a <u>salt gland</u>.

3. <u>Sea turtles have flippers instead of claws, and sea turtles cannot pull their heads and appendages completely into their shells like land turtles can.</u>

4. <u>Their eggs are exposed to a lot of danger, as are their young when they hatch.</u> As a result, many eggs must be laid to make sure that a few turtles survive.

5. <u>In sea snakes, the tail is laterally flattened rather than round, as it is in land snakes.</u> This aids the sea snake in swimming.

6. <u>No.</u> The only time a male sea turtle is on shore is when it hatches out of its nest. In adults, only the *females* return to shore, and that is only to lay their eggs.

7. <u>No. There was no new genetic information introduced into the population. The birds simply adapted to their different environments.</u> In the north, birds that had the right combination of genes that resulted in larger bodies were more likely to survive. In several generations, then, they became the dominant form of the species. In the south, there was no benefit to being larger-bodied, so that combination of genes was no more likely to survive than any other combination of genes.

8. <u>They are endothermic,</u> meaning they can regulate their body temperatures despite the temperature of their surroundings. The ability to fly also makes them very mobile.

9. <u>The physical features are present for a purpose and give scientists clues to their feeding behavior.</u> For example, straight, pointed beaks are helpful for diving birds because they move more smoothly through the water. Hooked beaks are helpful for grasping and tearing food. Webbed feet aid in swimming.

10. Since the bird has a pair of air tubes on its beak, it is most likely part of the group I called "shearwaters and similar birds." These birds spend most of their time on the open ocean and come to land only to breed. Thus, <u>it is either breeding or getting ready to breed.</u>

11. <u>The heavier bone came from the penguin.</u> Penguin bones are not hollow like those of the birds that fly. Thus, they are heavier. Of course, you could also break open the bones and look inside. The hollow one came from the gull.

12. <u>Look at the webbing on its foot</u>. The pelican will have webbing between all toes, while the albatross will not have webbing between the third and fourth toe.

13. The orders are <u>Cetacea, Pinnipedia, and Sirenia</u>.

14. The two groups of whales are the <u>toothed whales and the baleen (toothless) whales. Dolphins belong to the toothed whale group</u>.

15. The whale gulps large amounts of water into its mouth, and with its tongue, pushes the water against the baleen. <u>The baleen acts like a sieve to filter out plankton</u>.

16. The largest animal in the world is the <u>blue whale</u>, which is a member of order <u>Cetacea</u>.

17. <u>Whales do not have many calves</u>. A female may carry a calf for a year or more before delivering it and will not produce another calf for two more years afterward. This is a slow reproduction rate, and since some whales die naturally before they can reproduce, it takes a long time for whale populations to increase.

18. <u>Cetaceans have flukes on their tails, while sirenians have a square, paddle-shaped tail. Cetaceans have dorsal fins, while sirenians do not. All sirenians are herbivores, while many cetaceans are carnivores. Sirenians live in warm, shallow waters while cetaceans inhabit most waters</u>. The student needs list only two.

19. <u>Seals do not have external ears like sea lions. They also cannot rotate their anterior flippers backward or their posterior flippers forward</u>. So when they move on land, they must slink along the ground.

20. a. <u>blowhole</u> b. <u>nasal plug</u> c. <u>inner ear</u> d. <u>air sac</u> e. <u>melon</u> f. <u>lower jaw</u>

21. a. The blowhole <u>is the path for air to come in and out of the whale</u>. The whale needs the air to make the sound.

b. The nasal plug <u>controls pressure while the sounds are being made</u>.

c. The inner ear <u>receives clicks from the lower jaw and interprets them, sending signals to the brain</u>.

d. The air sac <u>muscles make the clicks</u>.

e. The melon <u>focuses and directs the clicks</u>.

f. The lower jaw <u>receives the clicks and sends them to the inner ear</u>.

22. <u>a. The oxygen supply is increased while oxygen consumption is reduced. b. Heart rate decreases and flow of blood moves to only the vital areas of the body. c. The rib cage collapses, forcing air away from the lungs so it cannot dissolve into the blood</u>.

23. <u>During breeding, a humpback whale will repeat its "song" over and over. These tunes are very specific to an individual, so scientists can often tell a specific whale by its song</u>.

24. <u>By being born tail first, the young can remain connected to the placenta longer</u>. This allows for a smaller chance of drowning during delivery. Upon birth, the calf needs to be quickly directed to the surface for its first breath of air.

25. <u>When a whale breaches, it jumps out of the water and then comes crashing back down into the water</u>. Scientists are not really sure why whales do this.

26. <u>A stranding of whales is a strange behavior in which one or more whales will swim to shore and strand themselves on a beach</u>. Once again, scientists are not sure why they do this.

27. <u>It is most likely less than a year</u>. Since the migratory marine mammals get to their breeding grounds once a year, they need to carry their embryo for a full year. Delayed implantation occurs specifically to lengthen gestation periods that are shorter than one year.

28. <u>No, it does not</u>. Because it is a filter-feeder, the baleen whale expends very little energy getting its food. A dolphin, on the other hand, has to hunt down its food. That takes a lot more energy. Baleen whales are generally much larger than dolphins and therefore need more food to support their size.

SOLUTIONS TO THE STUDY GUIDE FOR MODULE #8

1. a. Ecology – The study of the relationship between an organism and its environment

b. Abiotic – The nonliving part of an environment

c. Biotic – The living part of an environment

d. Carrying capacity – The largest population size that can be supported by a specific area with its available resources

e. Limiting resource – A factor required for a population to grow, but present in small quantities in an ecosystem

f. Detritus – Dead organic matter and the decomposing organisms living among it

g. Productivity – The rate of photosynthesis carried on in an ecosystem

h. Carbon fixation – The converting of inorganic carbon into useful organic carbon substances

i. Nitrogen fixation – The converting of gaseous nitrogen into useful organic nitrogen substances

j. Benthic – Describing organisms that live on the ocean bottom

k. Pelagic – Describing organisms that live in the water column away from the ocean bottom

2. Not necessarily. Within an ecosystem, there can be differences in abiotic factors, such as temperature, as you move up and down the water column. There can also be different concentrations of populations within an ecosystem, resulting in varied predator and prey numbers or competition for living spaces.

3. No. Populations need many specific resources to live. They must all be in ample quantities for continued growth. If even one element is lacking, growth cannot occur.

4. Intraspecific competition is when organisms of the same species compete for available resources. Interspecific competition is when organisms of different species compete for available resources.

5. The population of small fishes should rise. After all, the commercial fishing has reduced the number of predators. Thus, more of the small fishes should survive to the point where they can begin to reproduce.

6. The population will most likely shrink. If the surroundings change, the predator's camouflage is probably not suited to the area anymore. That will make it hard for the predators to get enough food. They will either move away or die.

7. The anemone and the fish appear to be in a symbiotic relationship. The anemone's stinging tentacles obviously do not affect the fish and probably provide it with protection from predators. The territoriality of the fish most likely helps ward off would-be predators to the anemone. This is possibly a mutualistic relationship.

8. <u>The marine biologist should look for parasites.</u> Since the fish that do reproduce are reproducing as much as ever, and since these fish aren't being eaten, they might be dying due to parasites.

9. There are several. The student need name only two:

<u>Zooxanthellae and coral</u> are mutualistic. The zooxanthellae produce food and other nutrients for the coral, and the coral provides food and a place to live for the zooxanthellae.

<u>Cleaner fish and shrimp are mutualistic with many fish.</u> The cleaner fish and shrimp clean their "clients" of parasites, and the cleaner fish get food. You could also have mentioned the specific case of the blue-streak wrasse and the oriental sweetlips.

<u>Clownfish and sea anemones</u> are mutualistic. The sea anemone protects the clownfish, and the clownfish lures food to the sea anemone.

<u>The coral *Pocillopora damicornis* has a mutualistic relationship with many creatures.</u> The creatures get shelter and hiding from the coral, and in return they protect the coral from predators.

10. <u>Yes. If the organism feeds both on primary producers, such as phytoplankton, and on primary consumers, such as zooplankton, it would be both a primary and a secondary consumer.</u> Most planktivorous organisms are technically both primary and secondary consumers. There are also some omnivorous organisms, feeding on nearly anything they find, that could be considered both as well.

11. Tertiary consumers feed on secondary consumers. Secondary consumers are the creatures that feed on those that eat the producers. Thus, tertiary consumers eat the creatures that eat the creatures that eat the producers. Thus, the <u>small sharks and juvenile groupers</u> are the tertiary consumers. They are also sometimes secondary consumers (when they eat the crabs or angelfish, for example).

12. <u>They break down the organic matter bound up in the producers' and consumers' dead bodies so that the material is again available to the ecosystem.</u>

13. <u>Not necessarily. There are marked differences of primary production among plankton.</u> As a result, primary productivity rates do not provide an estimate of phytoplankton concentration.

14. <u>Samples of phytoplankton and their surrounding water are taken at specific depths. These samples are placed in paired light and dark bottles.</u> The amount of oxygen in the light bottles represents the amount made from photosynthesis minus the amount used up in respiration. In the dark bottle, only respiration is occurring. Because of this, the oxygen level in the dark bottles is a result of respiration only. <u>The difference in the amounts between the paired bottles gives the oxygen amount produced by photosynthesis, which is a way to measure productivity.</u>

15. <u>An inorganic carbon source (like bicarbonate) with radioactive carbon is introduced into a sample from a marine system.</u> Only the producers can use that inorganic carbon, so <u>the amount of radioactive carbon that is used up from the inorganic source is a measure of the productivity</u>.

16. <u>The radioactive technique is better.</u> The light-and-dark bottle technique assumes that there are only producers in the samples taken. Any non-producers in the samples affect the results. Since only producers can use inorganic carbon, the radioactive technique deals only with producers.

17. Dissolved carbon dioxide gets into the ecosystem through respiration from the producers, respiration from the consumers, and the work of the decomposers. You might want to lump respiration into one group, but it is best to separate respiration of the producers from that of the consumers. It helps you remember that producers *do* use up oxygen and make carbon dioxide. There is an abiotic means by which dissolved carbon dioxide gets into the ecosystem. It can dissolve into the ocean from the air. However, the question asked specifically about biotic sources.

18. Blue-green algae are nitrogen fixers. They convert nitrogen gas into a useful form for the primary producers. Without them (and a few other nitrogen fixers), nitrogen would be unavailable to ocean organisms.

19. In bacterial denitrification, bacteria convert nitrogen molecules that they can use into dissolved nitrogen. This actually turns nitrogen into a less useful form, but the nitrogen-fixing bacteria will convert it into more biologically useful form.

20. Nitrates are the form of nitrogen used by most organisms.

21. Photosynthesis occurs in the photic zone.

22. No. Many benthic organisms begin their lives as plankton, floating with the currents as larvae, before they settle to a benthic lifestyle.

23. Even though it is not microscopic, it cannot swim against the flow of ocean currents (you learned that in Module #4), so it would be classified as a planktonic organism.

24. It lives in the inner shelf. Just saying the photic zone is not specific enough. I asked you to be as specific as possible.

25. It lives in the bathyal zone. Since it does not encounter sunlight, it is in the aphotic zone. Since it is nektonic, it does not live at the bottom of the sea, and since its depth varies greatly, it cannot live in the outer shelf, as the depth does not vary greatly there (see Figure 8.12).

26. It lives in the splash zone. If it lived in the intertidal zone, its feet would get wet walking on a shore that has recently been covered with ocean.

SOLUTIONS TO THE STUDY GUIDE FOR MODULE #9

1. a. <u>Intertidal zone</u> – The area of shoreline between high and low tides

b. <u>Substrate</u> – The bottom surface of a marine habitat

c. <u>Epifauna</u> – Benthic animals that move about the surface of the sea bottom, or are firmly attached to it

d. <u>Sessile</u> – A member of the epifauna that lives attached to a substrate

e. <u>Desiccated</u> – A term referring to an organism that has lost its body moisture

f. <u>Vertical zonation</u> – Noticeable horizontal bands of organisms living within a certain range in the intertidal zone

g. <u>Ecological succession</u> – A gradually increasing occupation of new organisms into a specific area

h. <u>Infauna</u> – Organisms that live under the sediment of an ecosystem

2. <u>The environmental conditions vary dramatically in the intertidal zone.</u> These varying conditions create lots of different ecosystems, which must be populated by lots of different creatures.

3. <u>Intertidal organisms are exposed to dry and wet conditions (based upon the tides), pounding wave action, and varying temperatures and salinities.</u>

4. Sessile organisms are firmly attached to a substrate so are <u>less likely to be tossed around due to the movement of waves.</u> But as a result, <u>they cannot move to a better location if conditions get bad.</u>

5. Some organisms can <u>move to moister, protected areas under rocks or in tide pools. Others can seal moisture inside their bodies.</u>

6. There may have been <u>rain (or possibly fresh water runoff from shore) during low tide, resulting in dilution of the water inside the tide pool.</u>

7. Some <u>store extra water and allow it to evaporate.</u> This cools them down like our sweat cools us down. Others have <u>shells of lighter color,</u> which help to reflect the sunlight so that it doesn't overheat them.

8. <u>Organisms in the lower areas are under water longer than organisms in the upper areas.</u> Since water contains the plankton and other things upon which many organisms feed, those that live in the upper areas have only a brief opportunity to feed.

9. <u>Since a sessile organism cannot move to look for a mate, the gametes must move in order to find another gamete to fertilize.</u> Planktonic gametes will move with the currents.

10. <u>As a wave reaches shore, the side closest to shore encounters shallow water first, hitting the bottom and slowing down. The other end of the wave continues at a faster speed, causing the wave to refract, or bend, until it is nearly parallel to shore.</u>

11. The area might be protected from strong wave action by <u>either an underwater canyon or a sand bar</u>. The canyon would divert the waves in a different direction, and the sand bar would receive the brunt of the strength of the waves (see Figure 9.5).

12. They produce <u>byssal threads</u>, which attach to the substrate. These threads start out as a protein fluid that forms into a strong, elastic thread when it mixes with seawater.

13. <u>They have to live on the bottom so that they can cling to the substrate.</u> As a result, they have no need to rise in the water column, which is what a swim bladder does for a fish.

14. <u>Predators can remove organisms, resulting in new space. Heavy surf from storms can wash away organisms or turn over the rocks on which they are living. Large, floating debris can crush organisms.</u>

15. <u>The upper limit of living space is determined by abiotic factors</u>, such as salinity, temperature, and moisture availability. <u>The lower limit of living space is determined by biotic factors</u>, such as predation and competition among individuals for space.

16. <u>The upper intertidal is sometimes called the splash zone because the main way it gets water is from the splash of ocean waves. It is sometimes called the *Littorina* zone because members of that genus are the most common organisms in the upper intertidal zone.</u>

17. There are many zones within the middle intertidal zone because <u>the water levels can vary dramatically, sometimes for many days at a time.</u> During neap-tide season, for example, the upper parts of the middle intertidal do not get water for many days at a time. When spring tide comes, however, that same part gets water during high tide. The organisms there, then, must be able to deal without water for a long period of time. The organisms in the lower portions of the upper intertidal will get water at least once a day, so they need not be as able to withstand long periods without water.

18. <u>Dryness determines how high the barnacles can live.</u> Barnacle larvae that settle too high in the middle intertidal typically die of desiccation. <u>Predation and competition determine how low the barnacles can live.</u> Once the barnacles get into areas covered by water most of the time, they have many more predators and have to compete with a lot of other organisms.

19. The area would <u>probably not be a climax community</u> because in the middle intertidal, the most common dominant organisms are mussels. Macroalgae and chitons typically represent the middle phase of ecological sucession.

20. <u>The rock with the algae was probably more recently cleared.</u> Mussels tend to be a climax community, which takes time to develop. Algae, on the other hand, can move in soon after an area has been cleared.

21. The <u>lower intertidal</u> has the most diversity because it is under water the longest of the three areas and therefore, more organisms can survive there.

22. <u>The limiting resource of the upper intertidal is water; the middle intertidal is space; and the lower intertidal are space and light. The dominant organisms of the upper intertidal are *Littorina* (periwinkles), the middle intertidal is dominated by mussels, and the lower intertidal is dominated by seaweeds.</u>

23. Sediment particles increase in size from <u>clay to silt to sand. Clay and silt together make up mud</u>.

24. The more the wave action, the larger the size of the sediment. Thus, in order of *increasing* wave action, you have <u>muddy, sandy, rocky</u>.

25. <u>They cannot live on top of the mud because the wave action pushes them away, as there is nothing on which to get a firm grip. They have to live near the surface of the mud because there is little water movement through the substrate and therefore little oxygen available</u>. If the organisms live near the surface, they can stick appendages above the surface and take in water when it comes to them. The water has oxygen dissolved in it.

26. You will find <u>anaerobic bacteria</u> there, because they do not need oxygen to survive.

27. <u>There are not many primary producers in the muddy intertidal. Thus, the organisms must eat detritus instead of primary producers</u>.

28. The <u>sandy intertidal will have greater zonation because it is more varied in its habitats</u>. In muddy areas, the bottom retains water despite the absence of the tide, so the type of habitat does not change much between the high and low tide marks.

SOLUTIONS TO THE STUDY GUIDE FOR MODULE #10

1. a. <u>Estuary</u> – A semi-enclosed area at the mouth of a river where fresh water and seawater meet and mix

b. <u>Euryhaline</u> – Species that can tolerate a wide range of salinities

c. <u>Stenohaline</u> – Species that can tolerate a narrow range of salinities

d. <u>Brackish</u> – Water that is less salty than seawater but saltier than fresh water

e. <u>Wetlands</u> – Estuarine areas of high elevations that are periodically covered with water

f. <u>Mudflats</u> – Wide expanses of an estuary that are exposed during low tide

g. <u>Meiofauna</u> – Microscopic organisms living in between marine sediment particles

h. <u>Channels</u> – Estuarine areas where water is present both during high and low tides

2. <u>The melting of large masses of ice after an ice age</u> caused worldwide ocean levels to rise, resulting in the formation of the most common type of estuaries.

3. The three types of evidence discussed in this course were <u>glacial deposits, large boulders that were clearly transported to their current location, and geological features such as deep lakes that are best described by the action of glaciers.</u> All these occur in areas that are temperate today, but they give evidence that at one time these areas were covered by glaciers.

4. <u>The uniformitarian thinks that several ice ages occurred throughout earth's history and that they all came and ended rather slowly. The catastrophist thinks that there was only one ice age, and it came about very quickly.</u>

5. Basically, you need <u>wet winters that are not too cold, and cooler summers that do not allow for a lot of snow to melt.</u> You can describe this in many ways, such as warmer oceans (that would lead to wet winters) or extra snowfall (which requires wet and not-too-cold winters).

6. The most common type is a <u>drowned river valley</u>.

7. <u>Fjords</u> have water that is most similar to non-estuary coastal waters.

8. A shallow estuary has <u>fluctuating salinity due to evaporation plus the mixing of fresh river water and salty ocean water; shallow water would result in higher temperatures; suspended sediments will make the water less clear.</u>

9. Think of the salt wedges in Figure 10.6. At a given point on the substrate, the salinity gets higher when <u>high tide</u> brings seawater into the estuary.

10. Once again, think of the salt wedges in Figure 10.6. The lines of salinity delineation tilt so that as you rise to shallower depths, you experience <u>decreasing salinity</u>.

11. The gyres in the ocean bend the outflow of a river in one direction, enabling marine organisms to live farther upriver on the opposite side.

12. In this situation, the left side of the river has higher salinity, because a stenohaline saltwater organism needs high salinity. This means the low-salinity side is the right side. Based on our rule, then, this must be in the Northern Hemisphere.

13. The finer sediments can travel farther in a river. Thus, muddy sediments tend to get deposited in an estuary.

14. It must be euryhaline because it can tolerate the wide range of salinities within an estuary.

15. Because osmoregulators are able to regulate their own internal solute concentration, they are less affected by salinity changes and are therefore more prevalent in estuaries.

16. The middle of the estuary has strong changes in salinity, so the creature must be able to reduce exposure to the water. Bivalves can do this by shutting down during salinity changes, and bivalves as well as other creatures can do this by burrowing into the muddy substrate.

17. Brackish water is a mixture of salt water and fresh water. Thus, look for brackish water species to find the center of the estuary.

18. It is most likely a salt marsh.

19. The red mangrove has prop roots to support the plant up out of the water and is therefore tolerant of high salinities. The black mangrove has pneumatophores that grow out of the soil for more exposure to oxygen but is less tolerant of high salinities than the red mangrove. The white mangrove has two salt glands at the base of its leaves to excrete excess salts and is the least tolerant of high salinities.

20. The lower the elevation, the higher the salinity. Thus, you will find red mangroves first, black mangroves second, and white mangroves last.

21. Cord grass is the common grass in a salt marsh.

22. Diatoms and other photosynthesizing plankton are the major primary producers in mudflats.

23. There is plenty of life in an estuarine mudflat. The major primary producers are microscopic (diatoms and bacteria), and most of the other organisms living there are buried in the muddy sediment.

24. Suspended sediments in the water clog the filtering organs of filter feeders, but there are plenty of deposits on the surface of the mud for deposit feeders.

25. Predators are present equally in both. At high tide, fishes come in to feed, and at low tide, birds and land animals have access to the exposed substrate.

26. The large populations of infauna combined with the varying depths at which they are buried keep the birds (with varying bill lengths depending on species) from overfeeding.

27. Estuaries do not have a large number of species, but they *do* have a large number of organisms living there.

28. You tend to find them in the channels, because that's the portion always covered by water, the food is ample, and there is good protection from predators there.

Answers to the questions in Experiment 10.1

a. By knowing the habitat preferences of the three types of mangroves, it should be fairly easy to determine the elevation of the land of the mangrove forest in the experiment. Since white mangroves are least tolerant to water, Transect #1 has the highest elevation, because it is the only one with white mangroves.

b. Because red mangroves are the most water tolerant (growing directly in salt water), Transect #2 has the most water-covered area, as it has the most red mangroves growing along it. This means it will have the most marine organisms.

c. Because Transect #3 alternates between red and black mangroves twice, you could determine that the land elevation becomes higher, then shallower (supporting red mangrove growth again), then higher yet again along this transect.

SOLUTIONS TO THE STUDY GUIDE FOR MODULE #11

1. a. <u>Corallite</u> – The cup-shaped calcium skeleton in which a coral polyp sits

b. <u>Septa</u> – A series of sharp ridges radiating from the center of a corallite cup

c. <u>Columella</u> – Central projections from the floor of a corallite cup

d. <u>Fringing reef</u> – A type of coral reef that forms as a border along the coast

e. <u>Barrier reef</u> – A type of coral reef that occurs at a distance from the coast

f. <u>Atoll</u> – A ring of coral reef with steep outer slopes, enclosing a shallow lagoon

2. Corals need <u>warm water, a hard substrate, and sunlight</u> in order to grow.

3. Encrusting <u>coralline algae</u> also aid in reef building. They do this by <u>growing over and trapping soft sediments and rubble, creating a new layer of hard substrate</u>.

4. a. Although it is a coral, soft coral does not form a calcium carbonate exoskeleton. Thus, it is a <u>reef inhabitant</u>, not a reef builder.

b. Hard coral is a major <u>reef builder</u>.

c. Coralline algae is another <u>reef builder</u>

d. Coral grouper live among the corals but do not add to the structure of the reef. Thus, they are <u>reef inhabitants</u>.

e. Crabs live among the corals but do not add to the structure of the reef. Thus, they are <u>reef inhabitants</u>. You could legitimately call them reef builders to some degree, however, as their molted exoskeletons do often add to the buildup of materials on the reef.

5. Corals belong in <u>phylum Cnidaria, class Anthozoa</u>.

6. <u>Soft corals are in subclass Alcyonaria, and stony corals are in subclass Zoantharia.</u>

7. a. <u>tentacles</u> b. <u>mouth</u> c. <u>septa</u> d. <u>columella</u> e. <u>nematocysts</u> f. <u>coenosarc</u> g. <u>gut cavity</u> h. <u>corallite</u>

8. <u>The broken pieces of coral can continue to grow and create a new reef structure, thus expanding the overall reef's size.</u>

9. <u>Coral can asexually reproduce upwards by moving up and secreting an elevated bottom and extended sides of the corallite. Coral can also grow laterally by budding off a portion of their body and secreting a new corallite. And finally, a new coral colony can begin when a piece of existing live coral is broken off.</u>

10. Two possible benefits of mass spawning are <u>(1) the large quantity of gametes provides more opportunity for survival from predators and (2) seasonal currents may be more beneficial to planktonic larvae.</u>

11. <u>When coral polyps reproduce mostly vertically, the resulting formation is a branching coral. When polyps reproduce mostly horizontally, the result is encrusting or boulder corals. And when there are nearly equal directions of reproduction, the coral is foliacious.</u>

12. <u>Mucus moves food particles toward a coral's mouth opening and moves trapped sediments off a coral's body.</u>

13. Coral can get food from the <u>photosynthesis of the zooxanthellae</u>, they can also get it by <u>trapping and eating plankton</u>, and they can also <u>extend coiled filaments from their gut to digest food particles</u>.

14. The three major areas of a fringing reef are the <u>reef flat, the reef crest, and the reef slope</u>. The <u>reef crest</u> is usually where coral growth is most prolific.

15. Spurs and grooves are most likely caused by <u>strong wind and wave movement</u>.

16. A barrier reef also has <u>a back reef slope, a lagoon, and possibly a sand cay</u>.

17. These underwater atolls at one time must have been growing near the surface of the ocean. What most likely happened is that the <u>volcanic base on which they are growing sank more quickly than the speed of coral growth, bringing the coral down below the photic zone so it could no longer live. Or the ocean levels may have risen more quickly than the coral could grow, again causing the coral to be too deep for light penetration.</u>

18. Spur-and-groove formations and algal ridges would be found on the <u>windward</u> side of an atoll <u>because this is the area of greater wind and wave action</u>.

19. <u>The coral reef efficiently recycles its nutrients and produces its own fixed nitrogen.</u>

20. Seaweeds do not overgrow a reef area because of the <u>nutrient-poor water and the constant grazing of reef fishes</u>.

21. Some corals use <u>digestive filaments</u> extended out of their gut cavities to digest the tissue of neighboring colonies. Other corals use <u>stinging tentacles</u> to injure their neighbors.

22. <u>It could grow over other corals, blocking out the sunlight and killing them.</u>

23. They form internal limestone spines called <u>spicules</u>.

24. We don't know for sure, but <u>soft corals are more susceptible to the plummeting of ocean waves</u>, and therefore bad weather might keep them in check. Also, <u>they require more optimal conditions to live</u>, so it is possible that suboptimal conditions keep them in check as well.

25. If organisms cohabitate, <u>the coral reef can provide living spaces for more organisms when they are sharing locations. This could nearly double the available living spaces for reef inhabitants.</u>

26. There are several:

Coral give zooxanthellae a safe home, and the zooxanthellae give food to the coral and recycle their wastes.

Remoras eat parasites off sharks, and the remoras eat the leavings of the sharks. The remoras are also protected, since most fishes avoid sharks.

Clownfish live protected in the stinging tentacles of a sea anemone, and the clownfish attract food to the sea anemone.

Several species of cleaner shrimp and fishes get some or all of their food by cleaning the mouths of predators.

Several species of shrimp, fishes, and crabs attack crown-of-thorns sea stars to protect the coral reef, and the reef gives them a safe place to live.

SOLUTIONS TO THE STUDY GUIDE FOR MODULE #12

1. a. <u>Benthos</u> – Marine organisms that live on the sea bottom

b. <u>Nekton</u> – Marine organisms that swim strongly enough to move against the ocean current

c. <u>Plankton</u> – Marine organisms that cannot swim strongly enough to move against the ocean current

2. <u>Sand dollars and crabs are members of the benthos. Sharks are members of the nekton. Larval fish and jellyfish are members of the plankton.</u> Remember, larvae generally cannot swim strongly if at all, so they are plankton.

3. <u>It stays underwater regardless of the tides.</u>

4. <u>Heavy wave action washes away fine particles and leaves mainly sand. Areas without much wave action, or those protected from it, have fine sediments.</u>

5. <u>Infaunal organisms</u> live buried in the sediment, <u>epifaunal organisms</u> live on the surface of the sediments, and <u>meiofaunal organisms</u> live in between the sediment particles.

6. <u>A muddy bottom substrate</u> contains little oxygen and lots of organic matter.

7. Because the physical conditions do not change as drastically as they do in estuaries, <u>soft-bottom shelf communities</u> have a larger number of species living in them.

8. <u>The infauna are not evenly spaced in the substrate of soft-bottom shelf communities.</u> They tend to clump together, and the reasons for this are not completely understood at this time.

9. <u>Detritus</u> is the major food source in the soft-bottom shelf communities.

10. It stands for <u>self-contained underwater breathing apparatus.</u>

11. <u>Most of the organisms in a sandy-bottom shelf community will use suspension feeding.</u> They would not be as prevalent in muddy-bottom communities because the fine particles in the water would easily clog their filtering mechanisms.

12. <u>Meiofauna are small enough to fit in between the individual particles of the substrate.</u> Thus, they do not have to dig into the substrate. They actually move in between the particles of the substrate.

13. <u>Suspension feeders do not like living near deposit feeders, because deposit feeders churn through the sediments looking for food.</u> This clogs up their food-gathering systems. Thus, it is rare to find them living together. <u>It is also rare to find them in equal numbers.</u> Generally, suspension feeders are more prevalent in sandy substrates, while deposit feeders are more prevalent in muddy substrates.

14. <u>In the tropics, turtle grass is most commonly found, while in temperate areas eelgrass is more common.</u>

15. <u>Many organisms feed on the decaying seagrass. Seagrass roots aid in keeping the soft substrate more stable, seagrass blades provide shelter for many creatures, and the blades are locations on which both algae and organisms directly dwell.</u>

16. The major grazers are <u>manatees, nudibranchs, sea urchins, sea turtles, and a few species of birds like Canadian geese</u>. You only need to list two.

17. <u>Epifauna</u> dominate the hard bottoms. <u>This is because there is little soft substrate into which infauna can bury.</u>

18. <u>Seaweeds need a hard surface onto which they can hold, because they do not have roots that can anchor them to a soft substrate.</u>

19. Some seaweeds <u>have special chemicals that give them a bad flavor, some are leather-like, and others incorporate calcium carbonate into their tissues to give them a "hard-shelled" outer surface.</u>

20. Kelps need <u>sunlight; a hard substrate on which to attach; and cold, nutrient-rich water in order to grow.</u>

21. <u>A kelp bed has kelp that are not tall enough to reach the surface of the water, while a kelp forest is composed of kelp that grow all the way up to the surface, forming a canopy on the surface.</u>

22. The sporophyte generation is diploid, while the gametophyte generation is haploid. Thus, <u>the cells of the sporophyte generation</u> have twice the chromosomes of the cells of the gametophyte generation.

23. <u>You are looking at an individual from the gametophyte generation of giant kelp.</u> In their full-grown adult form, they are often microscopic.

24. <u>Brittle starfish live among the holdfast of kelps, octopuses live on the substrate between the kelps, fishes live up in the water column among the blades of kelp, and sessile suspension feeders live directly on the kelp stipes and blades.</u>

25. <u>During a sea-urchin population explosion, there is not enough drift kelp on which to feed. So sea urchins crawl along the bottom and eat the holdfasts of the kelps.</u> This causes the entire stipe and blades of the organism to float away, and the resulting large amounts of drifting kelp eventually die.

SOLUTIONS TO THE STUDY GUIDE FOR MODULE #13

1. a. Epipelagic zone – The area of the water column that extends from the surface down to about 200 m

b. Holoplankton – Species of zooplankton that spend their entire lives as plankton

c. Meroplankton – Species of zooplankton that spend only part of their lives as members of the plankton community

d. Neuston – Planktonic organisms living at the sea surface

e. Vertical migration – Daily movement of small marine animals between the photic zone and lower depths

f. Dissolved organic matter (DOM) – Organic material dissolved in ocean water

g. Microbial loop – The flow of energy in the epipelagic beginning with the phytoplankton, dissolved organic matter, and the smallest zooplankton, making energy available to the major food web

h. Upwelling – The process that carries colder, nutrient-rich water upward to a more shallow depth

2. Neritic water is the part of the epipleagic zone lying over the continental shelf, while oceanic water is the part of the epipelagic lying over the rest of the ocean.

3. The epipelagic zone overlaps with the photic zone.

4. The epipelagic zone is home to an incredibly large population of phytoplankton that produce enough nutrients for this zone as well as others below it.

5. There are two main ways this happens. Fishes can swim from the epipelagic to a deeper zone and be eaten there. Also, unused organic material can sink into a lower zone.

6. From smallest to largest, we have picoplankton, ultraplankton, nanoplankton, and microplankton.

7. Even though the tiniest of plankton have been discovered, scientists cannot say they *fully* understand the epipelagic because throughout history, and even today more and more new information is constantly being learned about the intricacies of creation. It would be extremely prideful (and most likely incorrect) to assume we have figured everything out.

8. Cyanobacteria are picoplankton that can fix their own nitrogen.

9. Coccolithophores cover themselves in such plates.

10. Copepods are the most abundant.

11. Larvaceans are surrounded by a covering of mucus that captures food as it passes through filters on their bodies. When the filters get clogged with debris, larvaceans shed their mucus coverings and grow new ones.

12. A pteropod has <u>a foot that resembles a pair of wings</u>. Their name means "winged foot." They are members of <u>phylum Mollusca</u>. If you remember back to your first-year biology course, you probably learned that a foot was one of the distinguishing characteristics of mollusks.

13. Phytoplankton would <u>never be members of the meroplankton</u> because <u>no phytoplankton species transform within their life cycles to a non-planktonic form</u>.

14. Most nektonic species are <u>carnivorous predators</u>.

15. <u>Sardines and anchovies</u> are small planktivorous nektonic creatures, while <u>baleen whales, whale sharks, and basking sharks</u> are large planktivorous nektonic creatures. You need name only one of each.

16. Organisms have physical features that <u>create drag</u>, or use oils or gas to <u>create buoyancy</u>.

17. Flattened shapes <u>sink more slowly than rounded shapes as a result of greater drag</u>.

18. It is probably a member of the <u>plankton because nektonic species need to be streamlined in order to swim well</u>.

19. Yellowfin tunas are silver in color to <u>blend in with the silvery-blue water around them</u>. They have a dark dorsal side to <u>blend in with the darker depths below when viewed from above</u>. Their pectoral fins are stiff and moon-shaped for <u>steering and maneuvering</u>. Their dark interior muscles <u>work more effectively for swimming</u> due to greater oxygen and warmth.

20. The <u>Portuguese man-of-war</u> floats on top of the water using <u>air-filled floats</u>. The <u>by-the-wind sailor</u> also has <u>an air-filled float</u> that behaves like a sail. The <u>violet shell</u> floats by using <u>air-filled mucus bubbles</u>. The <u>sea slug</u> stays on the surface by <u>swallowing a bubble of air</u>. You need mention only one organism and how it stays afloat.

21. Many epipelagic zooplankton undergo <u>vertical migration, diving down to great depths during the day in order to avoid predation and returning at night to feed</u>.

22. <u>Many epipelagic organisms feed at several trophic levels, there are many species that have a varied diet, many organisms change their eating habits throughout their lives, and there is a sub-food web that utilizes the DOM</u>, making its bound-up energy available to the rest of the food web.

23. <u>Scientists thought that there was nothing small enough to feed on DOM. They were wrong because their plankton collection techniques were not good enough to capture the ultra- and picoplankton that feed on DOM</u>.

24. The epipelagic <u>does not have the same primary productivity throughout the world because there are factors that affect light availability and nutrients in various areas</u>.

25. Nutrient-rich deep water moves to the epipelagic via <u>overturn and upwelling</u>.

26. In general, overturn occurs <u>at the polar latitudes during the winter</u>. Because of low light levels in the winter, however, <u>primary production is not boosted until spring</u>.

27. It is <u>low</u> because these areas are located in fairly warm latitudes where the surface waters do not cool enough for overturn or surface mixing.

28. Primary production is generally high along the coasts because <u>the winds and waves result in constant nutrient mixing</u>.

29. Along the equator, <u>equatorial upwelling</u> replenishes the nutrients in the epipelagic. Also, there is a lot of light there.

30. <u>Areas that experience regular seasonal storms may have lighter seasons during ENSO. Also, deserts often receive much-needed rain during these times. While common species may experience a population decline, other species may have opportunity to thrive.</u>

SOLUTIONS TO THE STUDY GUIDE FOR MODULE #14

1. a. <u>Mesopelagic zone</u> – The pelagic layer of the ocean where light can penetrate, yet without the intensity to support photosynthesis

b. <u>Photophores</u> – Organs that produce light

c. <u>Hydrothermal vent</u> – A hot, actively spreading rift zone where heated water spews up from the crust

d. <u>Bioluminescence</u> – The production of visible light by living organisms

e. <u>Chemosynthesis</u> – The making of organic material from inorganic substances using chemical energy

2. Organisms below the photic zone depend on organic material that was produced in the photic zone for their food. As food sinks, it is fed upon by the organisms living in the upper layers of the deep ocean, and this leaves less food for the organisms below. Thus, <u>as you go deeper and deeper in the ocean, there is less and less food to support organisms</u>.

3. The dividing line between warm and cold water is called the <u>thermocline</u>.

4. <u>There is enough light for the creatures in the zone to see one another, but not enough light to allow for photosynthesis.</u>

5. <u>Zooplankton</u> are common in the mesopelagic.

6. Ostracods are in class <u>Crustacea</u>. They are sometimes called "seed shrimp" because <u>their bodies are encased in a hinged carapace, so they look like a shrimp inside a seed shell</u>.

7. Most mesopelagic fishes are <u>smaller</u> than epipelagic fishes and have <u>photophores</u> located on their bodies.

8. Mesopelagic fishes have <u>broad feeding habits</u>, eating nearly anything that comes into their path.

9. Mesopelagic fishes that sit and wait have <u>watery flesh and lack a swim bladder</u>.

10. Such a fish probably uses <u>vertical migration</u> to get food. The swim bladder is used to change depths, which is important for a vertical migrator.

11. The <u>blue disk</u> would be easier to see. Since red light does not penetrate water nearly as deeply as other colors, there is almost no red light down in the mesopelagic. The red disk looks red because it reflects red light. If there is no red light in the mesopelagic, there will be nothing to reflect off the disk, so it will appear black. There is blue light in the mesopelagic, however, so there will be light reflecting off the blue disk.

12. Bioluminescence is used for <u>breaking up an organism's silhouette (camouflage), identification of like species for communication or mating, defense, and as a "flashlight."</u>

13. It is most likely missing luciferase, the enzyme that catalyzes the reaction between luciferin and oxygen. You might have thought to say oxygen, as that is necessary for bioluminescence as well. However, since the bioluminescent organisms we have studied are aerobic, such a creature would not be alive without oxygen!

14. The big difference is that light produced by bioluminescence is cool, while that produced by fire is hot. Organisms could not stand the heat required to produce light in that way.

15. Luciferin and luciferase in the water cause this glow. The reason the boats see it in their wake is that the water must be disturbed so as to mix the two chemicals so they can produce bioluminescence. The rest of the sea is dark because it is not being disturbed; thus, the chemicals are not mixing.

16. Because of the water pushing down from above, increased depth results in an increasing pressure.

17. In the absence of light, there would be no silhouette for ventral photophores to break up. Also, eyes would not be useful, with the exception of locating the bioluminescence of other individuals.

18. There are no vertical migrators in the deep sea. They cannot stand the variation in pressure that would be required for the vertical migration.

19. A hermaphrodite can mate with *any* other member of its species, as it can produce eggs and sperm. Being a hermaphrodite means the creature does not need to look for an opposite gender. It is able to mate with any member of the same species. This makes it easier to find a mate in a place where it is hard to find anything.

20. In male parasitism, the male attaches to the female and draws nutrients from her. Thus, he acts as a parasite. Since he is always there, however, it benefits the female, as she always has a mate.

21. Deep sea creatures live at great depths under great pressure. We either need to bring them to the surface where we can study them (which would kill them) or dive down to their depths (which would kill us!). Fortunately, with the help of submersibles and deep water cameras, we can begin to learn about deep sea creatures.

22. Any food that sinks past a pelagic organism is forever lost to it. But on the sea floor, food collects there until it is found.

23. You would find mostly meiofauna, as they are the largest animal group on the sea floor.

24. Bacteria break down the non-readily digestible skeletal remains. Meiofauna then feed on the bacteria and broken-down material, making these nutrients available to the rest of the deep sea food chain.

25. Yes, they can. They can eat fecal pellets that have fallen from the upper levels of the ocean.

26. As a general rule, deep sea organisms are smaller, because we assume that the scarcity of food makes it hard for a large creature to survive. We do not understand, then, how the very large creatures can survive in this ecosystem.

27. Both hydrothermal vents and cold seeps support deep sea chemosynthetic communities by bringing up chemical nutrients for chemosynthetic bacteria. <u>Hydrothermal vents have black smokers as a result of precipitation of mineral-rich vent water that includes hydrogen sulfide. They are also much warmer than cold seeps and are located at fast-spreading oceanic plates. Cold seeps have white smokers as a result of precipitation of mineral-rich vent water that includes light-colored dissolved zinc sulfides. They are cooler than hydrothermal vents and are located at slow-spreading plate areas.</u>

28. <u>Photosynthesis does take place in the deep sea, because hydrothermal vents produce blackbody radiation, which can be used for photosynthesis.</u> The light-collection efficiency of these photosynthetic creatures must be *very* high in order for this to happen.

SOLUTIONS TO THE STUDY GUIDE FOR MODULE #15

1. a. Clupeoid fishes – Small, plankton-eating fishes that travel in large schools

b. Gadoid fishes – Large, bottom-dwelling fishes

c. Renewable resources – Resources that can naturally replace harvested numbers

d. Nonrenewable resources – Resources that are not capable of replacing harvested numbers

e. Sustainable yield – The amount of individuals in a population that can be caught without reducing the size of the population or letting it grow

f. Mariculture – The farming and harvesting of marine animals and plants

2. Areas of coastal upwelling have a greater supply of nutrients to support animal life. Wide continental shelves provide excellent locations for large populations too.

3. Antarctica and some areas around the North Pole (you need mention only one) are rich in primary production and thus have a lot of food resources. The harsh climate, however, keeps us from harvesting those resources extensively.

4. Trawls capture gadoid fishes, which are bottom-dwelling (demersal) fishes.

5. The second largest marine food group is the shellfish.

6. Because of their small size, clupeoid fishes cannot be filleted. As a result, they are often ground into fish meal, which is used as a protein supplement for other foods.

7. Schooling fish are usually caught in purse seines, large nets that encircle the school and then close around it.

8. Longlines are made up of floating mainlines, extending for 100 km along the ocean surface. The main line has up to 2,000 equally spaced, vertical lines, each with baited hooks. The fishermen then move back and forth along the mainline, removing hooked tuna and rebaiting the hooks.

9. Gill nets will trap nearly *any* creature not small enough to fit through the net opening, and as a result, gill nets kill many fishes and marine mammals not intended to be captured.

10. Yes. Even if a resource is renewable, it can be harvested to the point of extinction.

11. If fisheries' catches exceed the "maximum sustainable yield" of a population, it results in "overfishing." The populations would be unable to reproduce in the quantities required to keep the population form shrinking.

12. With a minimum allowable size, redfish individuals are able to grow to maturity and have an opportunity to reproduce before they are captured. This increases the population size without having to completely ban the capture of the species.

13. <u>The student is not necessarily correct. Although overfishing is a possible cause, some fish populations go through natural cycles in size.</u> The student might just be seeing the "low population" part of the cycle.

14. An exclusive economic zone is an <u>offshore area belonging exclusively to the geographically bordering country</u>. That country has complete control of all those resources located within that area.

15. Marketing can convince people to eat marine creatures they would not normally think of eating. <u>This can reduce the demand for a species that has a dwindling population, replacing it with demand for a species that is plentiful.</u>

16. In closed mariculture, the environment is completely controlled. <u>This limits the types of species possible to farm; facilities and manpower are very expensive; organisms with varying food and habitat requirements during their life cycles are difficult to manage; parasites or diseases may suddenly occur.</u> (You need name only two.)

17. In open mariculture, the environment is not controlled. Thus, <u>weather, pollution, and changing seasons can adversely affect the process. In addition, the high concentration of organisms can cause nutrient buildups that result in harmful algal blooms. Finally, natural habitats often have to be destroyed to make room for open mariculture facilities.</u> (You need name only two.)

18. Salmon are hatched and raised through juvenile stages in the mariculture facility. They are then released into the river, where they migrate out to the ocean. <u>They return to the facility fully grown and ready to spawn, after which they are conveniently collected by the mariculture farmers.</u> This "seeding" process is much less expensive for the facility.

19. <u>Manganese</u> is the non-renewable resource, because the others are living organisms that can reproduce.

20. <u>Oil, energy, various minerals, and water</u> are all nonliving resources in the ocean.

21. <u>Desalinization</u> is the process that removes salts out of seawater.

22. Dissolved substances can be removed from ocean water by <u>distillation or reverse osmosis. The latter has fewer drawbacks than the former.</u>

23. Energy can be harnessed from <u>tides, waves, and currents</u>, converting mechanical energy into electrical energy.

BLANK WORLD MAP FOR "EXPERIMENT" 15.1

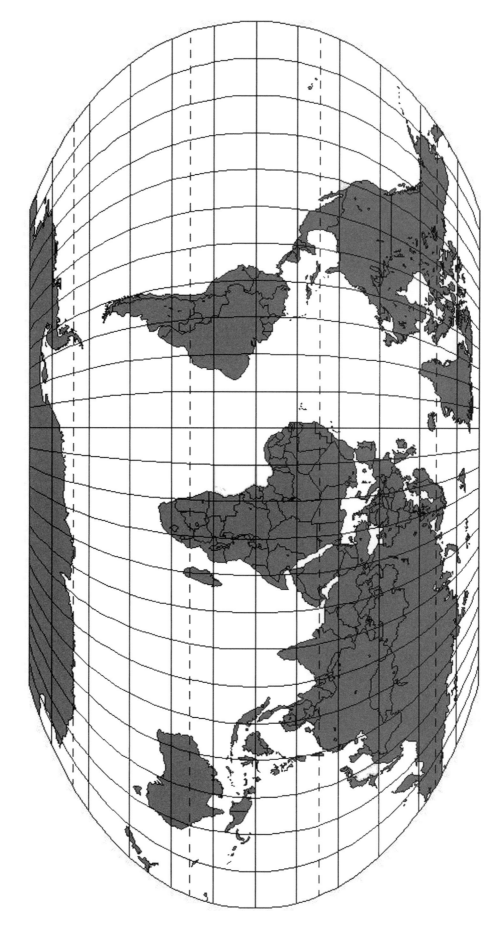

SOLUTIONS TO THE STUDY GUIDE FOR MODULE #16

1. a. Eutrophication – Excessive algal growth as a result of increased nutrient input

b. Nonbiodegradable – Substances that cannot be broken down by bacteria or other organisms

c. Biomagnification – The increasing concentration of a substance from one trophic level to the next

d. Fouling organisms – Organisms that live attached to surfaces that are under water, causing negative effects to ships and pilings

2. A direct effect on a habitat is a change that is caused at the time of the activity. An indirect effect on a habitat is when a change occurs as a result of an earlier activity or when a change occurs in a different location than that of the affected area.

3. Many materials can be carried to the ocean via waterways, trickling down through the earth, and even floating in the air.

4. There are many such effects: (1) Runoff containing excess nutrients can cause algal blooms that block sunlight from reef environments or pollute the water with toxic algal byproducts. (2) Fewer natural coastal areas cause increased erosion, resulting in extra sediments getting into the water. This prevents sunlight penetration and smothers existing corals. In addition, new coral polyps cannot settle onto the resulting soft substrate, and therefore the reefs cannot grow. (3) Explosives are often used to capture fishes in areas of coral reefs, damaging the reefs. (4) Explosives are also used to harvest coral as a construction material, for military operations, and to open areas not navigable by boat. (5) Divers that use poisons to stun and capture reef fish. (6) Uninformed sport divers can harm reefs simply by touching them. You need mention only three.

5. Bleaching is when corals spontaneously throw off a majority of their symbiotic zooxanthellae, resulting in a whitish color on their surface. It is an indication that the coral is under stress and vulnerable to disease.

6. Not all pollution is a result of man's activities. Some pollution is caused by natural occurrences such as volcanic eruptions and deep ocean seeps.

7. Because it is like detritus material, sludge can be used as fertilizer or can be pumped to marshes where bacteria in the mud can break down the organic matter.

8. The treated sewage contains chlorine, which is deadly to many marine organisms. It is good that the bacteria are gone, but since the chlorine that kills them also kills marine organisms, it is not clear that treated sewage is any better than untreated sewage as far as the ocean organisms are concerned.

9. Farming can cause eutrophication. The fertilizers and wastes that run off farms and into the ocean contain nutrients that the algae can use to bloom.

10. Remember that the rocky intertidal has more wave action than an estuary. Thus, the estuary will be most affected by the spill because it does not have very strong wave and tidal actions to aid in oil dispersion.

11. Oil flows into the ocean naturally through seeps. Oil flows up from the earth's crust through the seeps and into the ocean.

12. Human activities put oil into the ocean in several ways: (1) Offshore oil-well blowouts, (2) supertanker accidents, (3) city and parking-lot runoff, (4) underground storage-tank release, and (5) bilge-water release from boats.

13. DDT and PCBs are chlorinated hydrocarbons.

14. By testing the fishes for the presence of this chemical regularly, you can find out whether it is building up in their tissues over time or being broken down. Alternatively, if the predators of these affected fishes have the chemical in their bodies in greater concentrations than the original fishes, it is exhibiting biomagnification, which means it is not biodegradable.

15. We know that DDT travels throughout the world because it exists in virtually all parts of the biosphere despite the fact that it is human-made and was only used in certain areas of the world.

16. The marine biologists know that biomagnification increases the concentration of fat-soluble, nonbiodegradable chemicals as they travel up the trophic pyramid. Since marine mammals occupy the top trophic levels, biomagnification produces high concentrations in them.

17. Chemicals that bioaccumulate (build up in the tissues of organisms) show up in the tissues of their predators in greater concentrations (magnify) as the predators feed on more and more tainted organisms. Without bioaccumulation, there would not be biomagnification.

18. Nonbiodegradable chemicals are not able to be broken down by biological processes, and fat-soluble chemicals are stored in the fat cells of organisms. So the combination of these two means that chemicals remain stored in the tissues of affected organisms and remain in the food web.

19. Because these fish are at the top of the trophic pyramid, they have the highest concentrations of mercury. Mercury exposure in small quantities is not dangerous, and most fish have only small quantities of mercury in their bodies. Fish very high on the trophic pyramid, however, have higher quantities because of biomagnification.

20. It is important to keep fouling organisms off ships because they disintegrate ship hulls and add to the drag the ships experience. This indirectly results in more pollution. After all, if a ship's hull is destroyed, it must be rebuilt, which takes energy and makes pollution. In addition, increased drag results in the use of more fuel, which causes more pollution.

21. Radioactive waste is dangerous to nearly all living things, and potentially can remain toxic for millions of years.

22. It is nonbiodegradable and resembles living organisms such as jellyfishes. As a result, it will remains in the ocean without deteriorating and could tempt an animal to eat it and possibly die from the complications.

23. The welfare of people must be kept in mind. Many people depend on the ocean in several ways, and restricting their use of the ocean can result in suffering or death. In the same way, pollutants foul marine ecosystems, but many of those pollutants are the result of processes that save lives. We cannot

sacrifice the lives of people over those of marine organisms. We have to find ways to care for marine ecosystems that do not interfere with the health of people.

24. They are trying to make <u>artificial reefs</u>. The hard surfaces of the boats, planes, and cars provide substrate for coral larvae, promoting the formation of a new coral reef.

Answers to the Module Summaries in Appendix B

Not all of the blanks have to be filled in with exactly the phrases used here. As long as the general message of each paragraph is the same, that's fine.

ANSWERS TO THE SUMMARY OF MODULE #1

1. The 4 large ocean basins of the world are the <u>Arctic Ocean</u>, the <u>Indian Ocean</u>, the <u>Atlantic Ocean</u>, and the <u>Pacific Ocean</u>.

2. The part of the earth's crust that is covered with ocean is made up of <u>oceanic</u> crust. This is composed mainly of <u>basalt</u>, which is relatively dense solidified lava. The part of the earth's crust that is not covered with ocean is made up of <u>continental</u> crust. It is composed mainly of <u>granite</u>, which is less dense than the crust under the ocean.

3. The crusts float on the earth's <u>mantle</u>. The slow-flowing material that makes up the mantle is called <u>plastic rock</u> because it sometimes behaves like liquid and sometimes behaves like solid.

4. Scientists hypothesize that all the continents of the world were once part of a large supercontinent called <u>Pangaea</u>. The plates of the earth's crust are believed to have drifted to their present locations via a process known as <u>plate tectonics</u>.

5. There are two types of geological structures where two plates meet: a <u>mid-ocean ridge</u> system, where two plates move away from each other via the process called <u>seafloor spreading</u>; and a <u>trench</u> system, where two plates move towards each other, one dipping down into the mantle. This process is called <u>subduction</u>.

6. The geologic activity most commonly found around ridge systems is in the form of <u>earthquakes</u>, and the geologic activity most often found around trench systems is in the form of <u>volcanoes</u>.

7. Oceanic crust formation mostly occurs in the <u>Atlantic Ocean</u> where there is a large mid-ocean ridge. Oceanic crust is destroyed mostly in the <u>Pacific Ocean</u> where there are more deep ocean trenches.

8. The gently sloped shallow section of the edge of a continent is called the <u>continental shelf</u>. This location is where most ocean life is found. The <u>shelf break</u> is located at the point where the slope of the bottom begins to become steeper. The steeper section of a continental edge is called the <u>continental slope</u>. It reaches down to a gently sloping area at the base called the <u>continental rise</u>, where debris and sediment collect. The deepest region of the seafloor is called the <u>abyssal plain</u>.

9. The major property of water that keeps its molecules together is <u>hydrogen bonding</u>. This creates a flexible "skin" at the water's surface called <u>surface tension</u>.

10. Water naturally exists on earth in all three phases: solid – in the form of <u>ice</u> or <u>snow</u>, liquid – in the form of <u>water</u>, and gas – in the form of <u>water vapor</u>. When water freezes it becomes <u>less dense</u>, allowing solid water to float on liquid water.

11. Because water has a high <u>specific heat</u>, it does not change temperature very quickly despite drastic air temperature changes.

12. Because water can dissolve more substances than most other liquids, it is often called the <u>universal solvent</u>.

13. Seawater consists of pure water with materials dissolved in it. The solids come from <u>the weathering of rocks</u> on land, carried to the ocean by rivers. They also come from the mantle area of the earth, released through deep openings called <u>hydrothermal vents</u>.

14. <u>Salinity</u> is a measure of the total amount of salt dissolved in a solvent. Evaporation will result in <u>greater</u> salinity of the water left behind.

15. The ocean is blue because <u>wavelengths of blue light</u> can penetrate much deeper than those of the other colors. The blue color is enhanced by the reflection of the <u>blue sky</u> on the surface.

16. <u>Pressure</u> in the ocean increases dramatically with depth. For every 10 meters of depth, another <u>atmosphere of pressure</u> is added.

17. <u>Winds</u> in our atmosphere result from temperature differences caused by heat from the sun. They do not move in straight lines because of the <u>Coriolis effect</u>.

18. The major currents of the open ocean are driven by the wind. The circular patterns that result are called <u>gyres</u>. They move <u>clockwise</u> in the Northern Hemisphere and <u>counterclockwise</u> in the Southern Hemisphere.

19. Waves do not actually transport water, but they carry <u>energy</u> across the water's surface.

20. Tidal ranges are their largest during the <u>full moon</u> and the <u>new moon</u>. This is because of the gravitational pull of the aligned <u>sun</u> and <u>moon</u>. Scientists call this a <u>spring tide</u>. The smallest tidal range is when the moon and sun are at <u>right angles to each other</u> (during quarter moons). This is called a <u>neap tide</u>.

21. Cool winter temperatures cause the water temperature of the surface layer of the ocean to become colder, resulting in a <u>denser</u> portion of water. As this portion begins to sink, it displaces the same amount of water in a deeper layer. This process is called <u>overturn</u>.

22. The surface layer of the ocean is thin and well-mixed, being exposed to <u>wind</u> and <u>currents</u>. It is generally <u>warmer</u> in temperature than the rest of the water column. The <u>deep layer</u> is uniformly cold and much thicker than the surface layer. The <u>thermocline</u> separates them and is a transitional zone between them.

ANSWERS TO THE SUMMARY OF MODULE #2

1. For a definition of "life," we can say that all living things use <u>respiration</u>. They also <u>regulate</u> their internal environment and control the exchange of materials with their external environment. They <u>reproduce</u>, passing traits to their offspring to their offspring. They also <u>respond</u> and interact with external stimuli.

2. The process by which a living organism takes energy from its surroundings and uses it to sustain itself, develop, and grow is known as <u>metabolism</u>. Most of these processes utilize organic molecules from one of four main groups: <u>carbohydrates</u> – many of which are used for energy, <u>proteins</u> – some of which are part of muscle and other tissues, <u>lipids</u> – which are mainly for energy storage, and <u>nucleic acids</u> – which store basic genetic information.

3. Producers convert solar energy into a usable form via <u>photosynthesis</u>. Special pigments within these organisms, most commonly the pigment <u>chlorophyll</u>, absorb the necessary sunlight. The products of this food production from the sun are <u>oxygen</u> and organic matter in the form of <u>sugar</u>.

4. <u>Respiration</u> converts food into useable energy for an organism. This procedure produces water, carbon dioxide, and energy. Organisms that can make their own food are called <u>autotrophs</u>. Those that cannot make their own food are called <u>heterotrophs</u>. Organisms in this second group need to consume other organisms to obtain their <u>energy</u>.

5. <u>Autotrophs</u> must make more organic compounds than they need for their own metabolic process so that <u>heteroptrophs</u> can take advantage of the extra energy. The net increase in organic matter made by the photosynthesizers is called <u>primary production</u>.

6. The basic unit of life is the <u>cell</u>, and every living organism is made of one or more of them. The <u>plasma membrane</u> separates the internal fluid from the exterior environment, also controlling exchange of material going through it. Specialized membrane bound structures located inside, called <u>organelles</u>, are the site of many chemical processes such as photosynthesis.

7. The simplest cells, called <u>prokaryotic</u> cells, have no membrane bound structures. These creatures are commonly called <u>bacteria</u>. They have a <u>cell wall</u> outside the plasma membrane to provide support.

8. Most organisms in creation are <u>eukaryotes</u>, which means they have cells with many membrane bound <u>organelles</u> that perform a host of functions within the cells.

9. The levels of organization in living systems begin with the smallest unit of an element called an <u>atom</u>. A chemical unit that results from atoms bonding together is a <u>molecule</u>. A well defined structure within a cell is an <u>organelle</u>. The basic organizational unit of living material is a <u>cell</u>. A grouping of similar cells with a specific function is called <u>tissue</u>. When tissues perform as a unit, we call it an <u>organ</u>. An individual capable of reproduction is an <u>organism</u>. A <u>population</u> is a group of interbreeding organisms coexisting together. When integrated populations live within a limited area, it results in a <u>community</u>. A community, including the physical features of its environment, is called an <u>ecosystem</u>.

10. Marine organisms have to survive in a medium that could disrupt their internal metabolism, so they must maintain a fairly constant internal condition to survive. This process is called <u>homeostasis</u>.

11. When molecules move from areas of high solute concentration to areas of low solute concentration until there is an even concentration all around, it is called <u>diffusion</u>. The selectively permeable <u>plasma membrane</u> of a cell prevents large molecules from diffusing out. Smaller molecules like water, however, can pass through this selective barrier of cells. This process is called <u>osmosis</u>.

12. Organisms have several strategies to control the movement of water. Marine plants have rigid <u>cell walls</u> and a central <u>vacuole</u>, which cause pressure. Others, known as <u>osmoconformers</u>, adjust the concentration of dissolved substances in their body fluids to match the concentrations of dissolved substances in the water outside. Other organisms, the <u>osmoregulators</u>, maintain constant dissolved substance concentrations that are different from the surrounding environment.

13. Metabolic reactions usually proceed <u>slower</u> at lower temperatures and <u>faster</u> at higher temperatures. The body temperature of an <u>ectotherm</u> is completely determined by its environment. A <u>poikilotherm</u>, however, has a body temperature affected by its environment, but it has some mechanisms to control that temperature so its body temperature is not exactly equal to the environment around it.

14. When organisms have internal processes to heat their bodies, they are called <u>endothermic</u>. Animals like birds and mammals have nearly constant body temperatures and are called "warm-blooded" or <u>homeotherms</u>. Because most marine organisms are designed to survive within certain temperature ranges, temperature plays a large part in determining <u>where organisms live in the ocean</u>.

15. In reproduction, an organism must produce new individuals and transfer its genetic information to them in order to perpetuate the species. This transfer of genetic information is <u>heredity</u>.

16. When a single individual can reproduce itself without the involvement of another individual, it is called <u>asexual</u> reproduction. This can be accomplished by <u>cell fission</u> – where a single cell duplicates itself, <u>budding</u> – where portions of tissue are pinched off, or in plants, sending out <u>runner shoots</u> – to take root and form new plants. In all these cases the offspring are exact genetic <u>copies</u> of the parents.

17. When reproduction is a result of the union of gametes from two organisms, it is called <u>sexual</u> reproduction. The gametes are <u>haploid</u> cells, because they contain half the number of chromosomes in a typical cell. Fertilization results in a <u>diploid</u> cell, which is usually called a <u>zygote</u>.

18. When organisms reproduce by releasing millions of gametes, it is called <u>broadcast spawning</u>.

19. When scientists organize the types of creatures in creation based on their similarities and differences, it is called <u>classification</u>. A <u>species</u> is a population of organisms that have similar characteristics and can successfully breed with each other, producing fertile offspring.

20. All organisms are given two names in their biological classification – a <u>species</u> name and a <u>genus</u> name, the second term representing a more general grouping. This terminology is called <u>binomial nomenclature</u>, and it prevents the confusion that arises when common names are used.

21. When organisms are sorted into increasingly larger categories, it is called <u>taxonomy</u>. These categories, from the broadest to narrowest are: <u>kingdom</u>, <u>phylum</u>, <u>class</u>, <u>order</u>, <u>family</u>, <u>genus</u>, and <u>species</u>.

ANSWERS TO THE SUMMARY OF MODULE #3

1. Members of kingdom <u>Monera</u> are prokaryotic, single-celled, microscopic organisms. Even though they are the "simplest" of organisms, they have very <u>complex</u> cellular processes. The members of this kingdom are commonly called <u>bacteria</u>.

2. Most bacteria cannot produce their own energy to survive and are <u>heterotrophic</u>. The way they obtain their food is by breaking down either <u>the waste products of other organisms</u> or <u>dead organic material</u>. They are called <u>decomposers</u>. Their role in creation is very important because, without them, the important molecules incorporated in the debris they eat would be bound up in <u>dead material</u> forever.

3. Those bacteria that can produce their own organic compounds are known as <u>autotrophic</u> bacteria. Most of them use <u>photosynthesis</u>, getting their energy from the sun. Others utilize <u>chemosynthesis</u>, using the energy in stored chemicals such as hydrogen sulfide.

4. Blue-green algae, called <u>cyanobacteria</u>, are not true algae because they are prokaryotic. They utilize photosynthesis but do not have <u>chloroplasts</u>, which are organelles. When their populations undergo a bloom, the red pigments in their cells give the water a reddish color. This is called a <u>red tide</u>. These organisms can actually remove nitrogen from the <u>atmosphere</u> and use it in their metabolic processes. This is called <u>nitrogen fixation</u>, and it enables nitrogen to become a part of the food chain.

5. The plant-like organisms in kingdom <u>Protista</u> are commonly called <u>algae</u>. Algae are eukaryotic organisms that usually photosynthesize. They do not have true <u>leaves</u>, <u>stems</u>, or <u>roots</u> like plants. The unicellular organisms in this kingdom (plus those that photosynthesize in kingdom Monera) are called <u>phytoplankton</u>. They cannot swim faster than the <u>ocean currents</u> and therefore float along with them.

6. <u>Diatoms</u> are some of the most plentiful phytoplankton in the oceans. They are the greatest producers of <u>oxygen</u> on the planet. Their silicon dioxide <u>frustule</u> separates like a box and its lid in order to reproduce. When many of these silicon dioxide shells are deposited on the ocean floor it is called <u>diatomaceous ooze</u>. The dried deposits found on land are called <u>diatomaceous earth</u>.

7. Diatoms can asexually reproduce by <u>splitting their frustules</u> (which results in one of the offspring being smaller than the parent) or shedding their frustules and forming an <u>auxospore</u>. Diatoms sexually reproduce by forming <u>gametes</u> that make an <u>auxospore</u> after fertilization.

8. Dinoflagellates have <u>two</u> unequal flagella. Under the right conditions, these organisms can reproduce at tremendous rates, resulting in dense concentrations of individuals called a <u>bloom</u>. Some species release <u>toxic</u> substances that can cause the deaths of many organisms in the water around them.

9. Phytoplankton are nearly all microscopic. They basically swim in their nutrient supply, so nutrients can diffuse across their <u>cell membranes</u> and <u>wastes</u> can diffuse out.

10. The animal-like creatures in kingdom <u>Protista</u> are called protozoans. These organisms ingest food and are eukaryotic. Most are unicellular and are part of a group of organisms known as <u>zooplankton</u> that float with the ocean currents. There are two subgroups of this group: <u>holoplankton</u>, which spend their entire lives as plankton, and <u>meroplankton</u>, which are typically larval stages of organisms that can swim against the currents once they are mature.

11. The famous White Cliffs of Dover in England are made of foraminiferan tests which resulted from foraminiferan ooze that once blanketed the ocean floor. This indicates that at one time in history, this area was once the ocean floor.

12. Multicellular algae make up a third group in kingdom Protista. They are commonly called the seaweeds. These organisms have more complex structures than the unicellular algae and have more intricate reproductive strategies. Though many look like plants, they do not have true leaves, stems, or roots. Their complete body is called a thallus, which can have flattened, leaf-like portions called blades, bulb-shaped bladders for flotation called pneumatocysts, a stem-like stipe for support, and a root-like extension that behaves like an anchor called a holdfast. None of these structures transport materials through the body because each cell can absorb the nutrients it needs directly from the water.

13. The three types of algae (commonly known by their accessory pigments) are the green algae (phylum Chlorophyta), brown algae (phylum Phaeophyta), and red algae (phylum Rhodophyta). The cell walls of brown algae have an important substance called algin that is used as an emulsifying agent in food and man-made materials.

14. Diploid cells have chromosomes that come in pairs, while haploid cells have half the normal number of chromosomes (one from each pair). In seaweed reproduction, the diploid thallus has reproductive cells that divide by meiosis, resulting in haploid (1n) spores called sporophytes. Each then develops into a second generation thallus, but since no fertilization takes place, it is a haploid thallus just like the haploid spores. This haploid thallus is called a gametophyte generation because it produces haploid (1n) gametes. When two gametes come together, fertilization occurs, resulting in a diploid (2n) zygote. This grows into a diploid thallus known as the sporophyte generation (because it produces spores). This starts the cycle all over again. When a life cycle alternates between a sexual stage (gametophyte) and an asexual stage (sporophyte), it is called alternation of generations.

15. Organisms in kingdom Fungi have bodies made of long, thread-like tubes filled with nuclei. They do not have chlorophyll in their cells, however, so they cannot photosynthesize. Many behave like bacteria and decompose dead organic matter. Others exist with algae in a relationship known as symbiosis. This relationship results in a new organism called a lichen. The fungus provides support with its filaments, and the alga provides food produced from photosynthesis.

16. Members of kingdom Plantae are the true plants that have specialized structures such as leaves, stems, and roots. Seagrasses are the only marine plants that are completely marine. They send out horizontal stems along the sandy bottom from which vertical leaves emerge. Since they are under water, the male gamete (pollen) can travel with the water currents, so they do not need large, attractive flowers to draw pollinators.

17. Mangroves are salt-tolerant plants. They are found in the tropics and sub-tropics. The red mangrove can form dense forests along muddy shores. A unique feature of these plants is the presence of prop roots which trap sediments and build up more land area. Some types of salt tolerant plants remove excess salts from their cells using glands within their leaves.

ANSWERS TO THE SUMMARY OF MODULE #4

1. Kingdom Animalia contains the largest number of species and is split into two major groups: invertebrates (animals that don't have a backbone) and vertebrates (animals that have a backbone).

2. Sponges are in phylum Porifera and are composed of complex clusters of specialized cells. Water enters a sponge through pore cells and is pushed through canals because of movement from flagella located on collar cells. These cells also filter food from the water by trapping phytoplankton and organic matter. Sponges move the filtered water out of their bodies through the osculum. There are three basic sponge body types: ascon, sycon, and leucon. The cells of sponges have a remarkable "behavior" known as aggregation, where broken-off portions of the sponge body will come back together and reorganize, forming a new individual. For support, larger sponges may have a network of calcium carbonate or silica spicules that form a "skeleton." Often sponges have a web-like skeleton of elastic protein fibers called spongin. In the gelatinous layer located between the outer and inner layer of the sponge's cells, a number of wandering cells called amoebocytes secrete support structures, transport and digest food, expel wastes, produce gametes, and repair damaged portions of the sponge.

3. Sponges can asexually reproduce in three ways. The first method is when a portion of a sponge's body is broken off. The broken piece can grow into a separate sponge. A second way is through a process called budding, where an outgrowth pinches off so it is separated from its parent. A third way is by producing a group of cells surrounded by a shell made of spicules called a gemmule. This occurs during times of difficult conditions such as freezing temperatures. Because sponges are stationary organisms, it is beneficial for them to have sexually-produced planktonic larvae because the larvae can settle in other areas to avoid over-populating one place.

4. There are three types of body symmetry in creation: spherical symmetry – in which any cut through the organism's center results in identical halves, radial symmetry – in which any longitudinal cut through the organism's central axis results in identical halves, and bilateral symmetry –in which only one longitudinal cut through the organism's center results in identical halves.

5. Cnidarians exhibit radial symmetry. The mouth is on the oral side of the creature, and the side opposite the mouth is called the aboral side. The two basic body forms in this group are the polyp and the medusa. Both body forms have a centrally located mouth surrounded by food-capturing tentacles that have stinging structures called nematocysts. A cnidarian's gastrovascular cavity is not a true gut because it has no other opening except the mouth. Sexual reproduction among cnidarians results in a free-swimming larval stage, called a planula. Both cnidarian body forms can reproduce sexually, however, the polyp form is the only body form that can asexually reproduce by budding.

6. Most members of the cnidarian class Hydrozoa form colonies of tiny polyps. Some form drifting colonies of specialized polyps with flotation provided by a modified medusa that forms a float. The most well-known of these is the Portuguese man-o-war, which is often mistaken as a single individual instead of a colony.

7. Members of the cnidarian class Scyphozoa include the larger jellyfishes that spend most (or all) of their life cycle in medusa form. Even though jellyfish have a bell which enables them to swim, they cannot swim strongly enough to avoid the movement of currents, so they are technically plankton.

8. Members of the cnidarian class Anthozoa spend their entire life cycle in the polyp form. Corals and sea anemones are in this class. Coral polyps differ from hydrozoan polyps because they secrete

protective walls of calcium carbonate into which the polyps can hide. When the cup-like walls around each coral polyp remain attached, a coral reef is formed. Because coral polyps bud on top of older polyps, the outside of a coral reef is the only location where you will find living polyps.

9. Reef-building corals grow faster than other corals because of symbiotic dinoflagellates called zooxanthellae, which provide carbon compounds like sugars for the coral via photosynthesis.

10. Animals with bilateral symmetry have a dorsal (top or back surface) side and a ventral (bottom or belly) side. They are more active than most radially and spherically symmetric organisms and have a more complex nervous system to coordinate their locomotion. Animals in phylum Platyhelminthes are bilateral and are commonly called flatworms. Their brain is a collection of nerves in the head area.

11. The three types of symbioses are: mutualism (where all organisms benefit from the association), commensalism (where one organism benefits and the other is neither harmed nor benefited), and parasitism (where one organism benefits and the other is harmed).

12. Flukes are a type of parasitic flatworm. The adult fluke inhabits a vertebrate host, which must eat the organism that is host to the fluke's larvae in order to become infected. Tapeworms, another group of flatworms, are parasites that live in the intestines of many vertebrates. They do not have a gut or mouth, but rely on their host to digest food for them, which they absorb directly into their bodies.

13. A one-way digestive tract, such as that found phylum Nemertea, is a better arrangement than a single-opening tract because with two openings, a mouth and an anus, material can continue to move through the organism as it crawls through the sediments in which it lives.

14. Many members of phylum Nematoda live as parasites in host fishes. Their larvae are notorious for causing reactions among people eating raw fish.

15. Worms belonging to phylum Annelida have segmented bodies. They have a gut that travels the length of the body inside another body cavity called the coelom. This cavity is filled with fluid that supports the body's structure. When the body's muscles contract in sequence against the fluid's pressure, it results in an ability to move and squirm, but offers little control of movement.

16. Larger polychaetes cannot absorb oxygen directly from the surrounding water. They are equipped with gills which contain thin-walled blood vessels that allow for easy absorption of gases.

17. Lophophorates have a special structure for feeding called a lophophore, which is a crown of ciliated tentacles around the mouth. A main difference between lophophorates and the worms is that their gut is not straight but rather U-shaped.

18. Though lamp shells look like clams, they are not true clams. The shells of a lamp shell are located on the dorsal and ventral parts of its body, as opposed to a clam's, which are on the left and right sides. Lamp shells also have ciliated lophophores for gathering food.

ANSWERS TO THE SUMMARY OF MODULE #5

1. Most members of phylum <u>Mollusca</u> have a bilaterally symmetric, soft body protected by a shell made of calcium carbonate. The body is covered by a <u>mantle</u> which produces the shell and performs respiration. Many mollusks use a large, muscular <u>foot</u> for locomotion, anchoring, or obtaining food. They have <u>gills</u> for exchanging gases with the water and a <u>radula</u> that they use for scraping food.

2. Class <u>Gastropoda</u> includes limpets, conchs, and whelks. It is named for organisms displaying a <u>stomach-foot</u> body shape. Many species have a horny plate, called an <u>operculum</u>.

3. Class <u>Bivalvia</u> includes clams and scallops. It is named for the two hinged shells or valves on their bodies. To filter food and exchange gases, these organisms extend <u>siphons</u> to suck in and expel water. Some individuals in this class, such as mussels, have strong filaments called <u>byssal threads</u> that are used to attach themselves to rocks.

4. When a small piece of material gets caught inside an oyster's body, its mantle secretes <u>calcium carbonate</u> around the material. Layers and layers of these secretions finally produce a <u>pearl</u>. To culture these gems, small irritants are <u>manually</u> inserted into oysters to cause irritation.

5. Class <u>Cephalopoda</u> includes squids and octopuses. It is named for those organisms displaying a <u>head-foot</u> body shape. Cephalopods are predators with sucker-lined <u>tentacles</u>, well-developed sense organs, and relatively large <u>brains</u>. Many can camouflage using <u>chromatophores</u> that change colors. Since cephalopods are <u>active</u>, they need a circulatory system unaffected by gravity. They therefore have a <u>closed circulatory system</u> in which the blood is always in vessels. Because an octopus has no <u>shell</u>, it can forcefully contract its <u>mantle cavity</u> to shoot out a jet of water, propelling it backward.

6. Mollusks have a heart for pumping blood. Except for the cephalopods, mollusks have an <u>open circulatory system</u>, meaning that their blood does not circulate entirely within vessels, but sometimes it is released into open blood spaces where it comes into direct contact with the <u>tissues</u>. Most mollusks are <u>hermaphroditic</u>, meaning that each individual can produce both male and female gametes. With the exception of most cephalopods, fertilization is <u>external</u>.

7. Organisms in phylum <u>Arthropoda</u>, meaning "joint-foot," include shrimp, lobsters, and crabs. They are all <u>bilaterally</u> symmetric and are covered with a jointed suit of armor called an <u>exoskeleton</u> that is made of <u>chitin</u>. This outer covering cannot grow with the individual, so it must be shed so that the organism can grow. This process is called <u>molting</u>, and the organism is <u>vulnerable</u> during this time.

8. Most of the marine arthropods are in the class <u>Crustacea</u>. Some of their more notable body characteristics include an exoskeleton, gills, special appendages for <u>swimming</u>, and two pairs of <u>antennae</u>. Their three body segments include a <u>head</u>, <u>thorax</u>, and <u>abdomen</u>. Many of the larger crustaceans have a <u>cephalothorax</u>, which is a fused head and thorax. The armor that covers this area is called a <u>carapace</u>. Most crustaceans do not broadcast their <u>gametes</u> into the water, but rather, the males will transfer sperm directly to the females who <u>store it</u> to later fertilize many batches of eggs.

9. Shrimp, lobsters, and crabs belong to the crustacean order <u>Decapoda</u>, meaning "10 legs." Crabs have a small abdomen folded under their larger <u>cephalothorax</u>. Females have a wider abdomen than males in order to <u>carry eggs</u>. Crabs can survive on land for long periods of time because their hard <u>exoskeleton</u> keeps moisture from escaping the body cavity, allowing the <u>gills</u> to stay moist. Creatures in the phylum <u>Echinodermata</u> include sea stars, sea urchins, and sand dollars. They are <u>radially</u>

symmetric, yet their larval forms are <u>bilaterally</u> symmetric. Their adult symmetry is called <u>pentamerous</u>, based on five radiating parts. The skeleton of echinoderms is an <u>endoskeleton</u> as opposed to an exoskeleton. They have a unique internal <u>water vascular system</u>, made up of a series of water-filled canals. This network is used for <u>locomotion</u> and <u>feeding</u>. The canals hydraulically operate numerous <u>tube feet</u>, which are extensions of the canals that extend for locomotion and sensory, respiratory, and excretory duties.

10. Among the echinoderms, sea stars, brittle stars, and crinoids have <u>simple, short</u> guts, but sea urchins and sea cucumbers have <u>long, coiled</u> guts in order to digest the plant and detritus they feed upon. Most echinoderms are separate sexes and <u>broadcast</u> their gametes directly into the water column. To increase the chances of finding each other, gametes are usually released in the <u>same relative time period during a short season of the year</u>. Also, individuals of the <u>same</u> species release their gametes when gametes of a like species are in the water. Each individual releases <u>an enormous</u> quantity of gametes, too.

11. All organisms in the phylum <u>Chordata</u> have at some point in their development a supportive <u>notochord</u>, which is a flexible supportive rod, running the length of their bodies. They also have a hollow <u>dorsal nerve cord</u>, which is a long bundle of nerve cells. And they have folds of skin, called <u>pharyngeal pouches</u>, along their neck during embryonic development. These often develop openings to allow water to flow over the gills, but in non-aquatic organisms, the folds of skin develop into various neck structures like the thymus gland.

12. <u>Tunicates</u> do not have a notochord in their adult form, but instead have a leather-like tunic covering for support. The <u>sea squirts</u> in this group are often mistaken for sponges due to their rounded appearance.

13. Lancelets have an <u>atrial cavity</u> that collects the water that the lancelet takes in for filtering and sends it out the body through the <u>atriopore</u>.

Identification

a. <u>umbo</u> b. <u>muscle</u> c. <u>mouth</u> d. <u>foot</u> e. <u>gonad</u> f. <u>gut</u> g. <u>heart</u> h. <u>muscle</u> i. <u>anus</u> j. <u>siphons</u> k. <u>gills</u> l. <u>mantle</u>

m. <u>water vascular system</u> n. <u>tube feet</u> o. <u>ampullae</u> p. <u>madreporite</u> q. <u>ambulacral grooves</u> r. <u>mouth</u>

ANSWERS TO THE SUMMARY OF MODULE #6

1. The three major types of marine fishes are <u>jawless</u>, <u>cartilaginous</u>, and <u>bony</u>. They have endoskeletons, which can <u>grow</u> with the creature, unlike exoskeletons.

2. Jawless fishes lack <u>jaws</u>, paired <u>fins</u>, and have no <u>scales</u> on the outside of their bodies. Instead of bones, their skeletons are made of <u>cartilage</u>, lacking <u>osteoblast</u> and <u>osteocyte</u> cells. Lampreys are hatched in <u>fresh</u> water, migrate to <u>salt</u> water when adults, and return to fresh water to <u>reproduce</u>. This type of life cycle is called <u>anadromous</u>.

3. Sharks' bodies are literally covered with teeth called <u>placoid</u> scales (or <u>denticles</u>). They often swim with their mouths open to aid in obtaining <u>oxygen</u> from the water. Shark species each have a unique <u>tooth</u> shape specifically designed for their prey. These structures are oriented in many <u>rows</u> and are replaced often. Some very large sharks with extremely small ones are <u>filter</u> feeders and are the largest fish species in the world.

4. The term <u>demersal</u> refers to a fish that lives on the ocean floor. Most skates and <u>rays</u> live on the ocean floor. Their eyes are located on the <u>dorsal</u> side of their flattened bodies so they can see predators above them. To crush the hard shells of their prey, they have a set of <u>plates</u> instead of teeth.

5. <u>Bony</u> fishes represent 98% of all fishes in the world. Their bodies are covered with thin, protective <u>scales</u> formed from bone. The two types of scales are <u>cycloid</u>, which have smooth, rounded edges, and <u>ctenoid</u>, which have comb-like extensions. Instead of the gill slits found in cartilaginous fishes, bony fishes have an <u>operculum</u> that covers and protects their gills. To control buoyancy in the water, bony fishes utilize a <u>swim bladder</u>.

6. A <u>tapered</u> body shape allows fishes to swim easily through the water. Other fish body shapes are perfectly suited to their habitats. The flounder has a <u>flat</u> body shape so that it can lay on its <u>side</u>, camouflaged with the ocean floor.

7. The three basic categories for the use of color in fishes are <u>camouflage</u>, <u>disguise</u>, and <u>advertisement</u>. One type of disguise, <u>countershading</u>, is when fishes exhibit a silver-white ventral side and dark dorsal side.

8. The parallel bands of muscle that contract in succession along the length of a fish's body are called <u>myomeres</u>.

9. Filter feeding fishes strain plankton out of the water using <u>gill rakers</u> located on the inner surface of their gills. The size of the spaces between the gill rakers determines the size of the <u>food</u> captured. Fishes that feed on plants and seaweeds are called <u>grazers</u>. They have <u>long</u>, coiled guts to process their food. Carnivorous fishes, on the other hand, have straight, <u>short</u> guts. Parrotfish are often called "<u>beach makers</u>" because they eat <u>reef corals</u> and pass the unused calcium carbonate material, resulting in a sandy substance.

10. Since sharks have no <u>swim bladder</u>, their large, oily <u>liver</u> aids in buoyancy. To save room in their bodies, they have a <u>spiral valve</u> instead of long, coiled intestines. This design increases <u>surface area</u> without taking up a lot of space.

11. Fishes have a <u>two</u>-chambered heart that pumps <u>oxygen-poor</u> blood to the gills. Since the blood flows in the opposite direction as the water moving past the gills, oxygen can <u>diffuse</u> into the blood along the entire length of the gill. This is called a <u>countercurrent</u> system of blood flow. Because water inhibits the penetration of light, fishes have relatively large <u>olfactory lobes</u> in their brains for a sharp sense of smell. They also have a sensory feature called a <u>lateral line</u>, made up of small canals found along the length of the body. Sharks have an added sensory feature, called <u>ampullae of Lorenzini</u>, which aids in the detection of the tiniest of electrical fields.

12. Fishes often aggregate into groups, called <u>schools</u>, when they are juveniles. This most likely offers them a degree of protection from predators. When large predators group together, it is often to corral <u>prey</u> for feeding. To follow the daily movement of plankton populations up and down in the water column, predatory fish will <u>migrate</u>. Some fish species spend their adult lives in fresh water and move to salt water for reproduction. These fishes' life cycles are called <u>catadromous</u>.

13. To increase the chances for reproduction, some fish species are <u>hermaphroditic</u>, changing gender if necessary. Spawning is a type of <u>external</u> fertilization employed by many fishes. When a female fish releases eggs that are fertilized outside her body, the eggs experience <u>oviparous</u> development. If fertilized eggs remain in a female's body and hatch there, this is called <u>ovoviviparous</u> development. Finally, when the young obtain nutrients directly from the mother and are birthed alive, this is called <u>viviparous</u> development.

Identification

a. <u>nare</u> b. <u>eye</u> c. <u>spiracle</u> d. <u>lateral line</u> e. <u>dorsal fins</u> f. <u>caudal fin</u> g. <u>anal fin</u> h. <u>pelvic fins</u> i. <u>pectoral fins</u> j. <u>gill slits</u> k. <u>mouth</u>

l. <u>heart</u> m. <u>liver</u> n. <u>kidney</u> o. <u>spleen</u> p. <u>rectum</u> q. <u>spiral intestine</u> r. <u>pancreas</u> s. <u>stomach</u>

ANSWERS TO THE SUMMARY OF MODULE #7

1. Marine turtles and birds remove excess salts from their bodies using a salt gland.

2. Sea turtles differ from land turtles in that they have flippers instead of claws and cannot pull their heads and appendages into their shells.

3. Sea turtle hatchlings experience many difficulties until they reach the ocean. They have to dig themselves out of their sandy nest, move in the right direction towards the sea, and avoid predation by crabs, birds, and fishes.

4. Sea snakes and marine iguanas differ from land species by the presence of a flattened tail that aids in swimming.

5. The sea turtle female returns to shore in order to lay her eggs. She lays several eggs to increase the chances that a few will survive the perils of youth and reach adulthood.

6. When a helpful trait is newly expressed by a species, it is called an adaptation. This "new" trait is not new at all but comes directly from the genetic information already possessed by the individual.

7. Marine birds are present in a wider array of sea environments than marine reptiles because they are endothermic and extremely mobile.

8. The shape of marine birds' beaks plays an important role in their feeding habits. For example, straight beaks are streamlined for diving.

9. Albatrosses and shearwaters spend most of their lives over water, coming to land only to reproduce. They have air tubes on the upper edge of their bills into which their salt glands drain.

10. Penguins typically live in and around regions of Antarctica. They have solid bones, enabling them to swim and dive more easily.

11. Pelicans are better swimmers than many birds because of webbing between all four of their toes.

12. The three orders of marine mammals are Cetacea (toothed and baleen whales), Pinnipedia (seals and sea lions), and Sirenia (manatees).

13. Dolphins are in the toothed whale group, while plankton-feeding whales are in the baleen whale group.

14. A baleen aids the blue whale in filtering plankton. The animal expends less energy collecting plankton than it would if it hunted prey.

15. Endangered whales cannot repopulate the oceans quickly because they do not reproduce often, and have long gestation rates.

16. Members of the orders Cetacea and Sirenia swim dorso-ventrally as opposed to fishes, which swim laterally.

17. Seals differ from sea lions in that they do not have <u>external</u> ears. They also cannot rotate their <u>flippers</u> in order to crawl on land.

18. When a dolphin echolocates, it moves air out of its <u>blowhole</u>. The <u>air sac</u> muscles make the clicks. The <u>nasal plug</u> controls pressure while the sound is being made, and the <u>melon</u> focuses and directs the clicks. The <u>lower jaw</u> receives the clicks and sends them to the <u>inner ear</u> which sends the signals to the <u>brain</u>.

19. During a deep dive, marine mammals increase their oxygen levels by <u>exhaling</u> as much air as possible at the water's surface in order to replenish supplies with <u>new, more oxygenated air</u>. Their <u>heart</u> rate decreases, and flow of blood moves only to the <u>vital areas of the body</u>. Finally, their <u>rib cage</u> collapses, forcing air away from the lungs so it cannot be dissolved into the blood.

20. Any activity an organism would do in its natural habitat is called a <u>behavior</u>. One common activity, called <u>breaching</u>, is when the animal leaps out of the water and crashes onto the surface.

21. Pinnipeds return to breeding grounds <u>annually</u>, however, they have a <u>gestation</u> period that is less than a year. To extend the time before a pup is born, the embryo stops developing for a few months until it finally <u>attaches to the uterine wall</u>. This is called <u>delayed implantation</u>.

22. Cetaceans breed and deliver their young in the water. The calves are born <u>tail</u> first so that they can remain connected to the <u>placenta</u> as long as possible. This decreases the chance of <u>drowning</u> during delivery.

23. During breeding, a humpback whale will repeat its "<u>song</u>" over and over, and scientists can often identify a specific individual by analyzing it.

Identification

a. <u>blowhole</u> b. <u>nasal plug</u> c. <u>inner ear</u> d. <u>air sac</u> e. <u>melon</u> f. <u>lower jaw</u>

ANSWERS TO THE SUMMARY OF MODULE #8

1. The study of the relationship between an organism and its environment is called <u>ecology</u>. The nonliving part of the environment is called the <u>abiotic</u> part and includes the <u>physical and chemical</u> features. The living part of the environment is the <u>biotic</u> part.

2. When organisms in an ecosystem reproduce under optimal conditions so that the number of new offspring is greater than the number of dying adults, the population undergoes an <u>explosion</u>.

3. The largest population size that can be supported by a specific area with its available resources is the <u>carrying capacity</u> of that area. All resources such as nutrients, light, and space must be present for a population to exist there. If one of these components is scarce or missing, it is called a <u>limiting resource</u>.

4. When individuals of the same species compete over available resources, it is called <u>intraspecific</u> competition. When two different species compete over available resources, it is called <u>interspecific</u> competition.

5. An organism's <u>niche</u> includes its feeding habits, requirements for a living space, reproductive strategy, and its behaviors.

6. Species can use strategies such as speed, defense, and hiding to avoid becoming <u>prey</u>. <u>Predators</u> use methods such as camouflage and lures to draw their potential food closer.

7. A close living association between 2 species is called <u>symbiosis</u>. The larger individual, usually called the <u>host</u>, lives in close association with the smaller individual, usually called the <u>symbiont</u>. When one species benefits from the relationship and the other is not affected, it is called <u>commensalism</u>. When one species benefits and the other is harmed, it is called <u>parasitism</u>. <u>Mutualism</u> is where both organisms benefit from living in close association with one another.

8. <u>Autotrophs</u>, such as algae, get energy from their environment and use it to make their own food. <u>Heterotrophs</u>, such as fishes, obtain their energy from feeding on algae or other species like themselves.

9. The trophic relationships in a food chain begin with the <u>primary producers</u> that make their own food. They are fed upon by the <u>primary consumers</u>. These organisms are then fed upon by <u>secondary consumers</u> which are preyed upon by <u>tertiary consumers</u>.

10. Since there is usually more than one type of primary producer, and there are many consumers that feed on more than one of them, a <u>food chain</u> does not accurately depict what happens in an ecosystem. A <u>food web</u> takes into account things such as organisms feeding on many types of other organisms and changing their feeding habits as they get older.

11. An <u>ecological pyramid</u> illustrates the fact that 80-90% of <u>energy</u> is lost from one trophic level to another. This is not lost to the ecosystem, however, because much of the unused energy is bound up in <u>detritus</u>, consisting of dead organic matter and the decomposing organisms living within it. Many organisms feed directly on this material, bringing the energy bound up in it back into the <u>food web</u>.

12. The rate of photosynthesis carried on in an ecosystem is its <u>productivity</u>. During photosynthesis, inorganic carbon is fixed into organic carbon via a process called <u>carbon fixation</u>.

13. The two ways to measure productivity are the traditional method, <u>the light and dark bottle technique</u>, and the more recent method, <u>the radioactive carbon technique</u>. The first method measures <u>oxygen</u> levels used by producers and indirectly determines production. The second method measures <u>radioactive carbon</u> levels and directly determines production.

14. Primary productivity does not necessarily determine the <u>population</u> of phytoplankton in an area. Some species may be highly productive while others may not.

15. In the carbon cycle, primary producers take dissolved <u>carbon dioxide</u> from the water and use sunlight and water to convert it into oxygen and <u>sugar</u>. This is known as <u>carbon fixation (or photosynthesis)</u>. The carbon, which is now part of an organic molecule, is eaten by <u>herbivores (or primary consumers)</u> which, in turn are eaten by <u>carnivores (or secondary consumers)</u>. At the same time, all of these organisms are burning their food for energy via <u>respiration</u> and are putting inorganic carbon back into the environment in the form of <u>carbon dioxide</u>.

16. In the nitrogen cycle, gaseous <u>nitrogen</u> from the atmosphere dissolves into the water where <u>some types of bacteria (or blue green algae)</u> convert it into usable organic forms. This process is called <u>nitrogen fixation</u>. Primary producers use these organic forms, especially in the form of <u>nitrate</u>, and pass them along the food web.

17. At the boundary between land and sea is the shallow <u>intertidal</u> zone. It is exposed to air at low tide and under water at high tide. Above this zone is the <u>splash zone</u> that is never under water but is exposed to salt spray. Below these zones is the <u>inner shelf</u> that is always underwater and is the area where light can penetrate through the water down to the sea floor. All three of these zones make up the <u>photic zone</u>, where light is intense enough for photosynthesis to occur.

18. All zones below the photic zone are in the <u>aphotic zone</u> where there is little or no light. The shallowest area here is the <u>outer shelf</u> that extends to the edge of the continental shelf. Where the continental shelf drops to the deep ocean is the <u>bathyal zone</u>.

19. Organisms that live on the ocean bottom are <u>benthic</u>. Organisms that live in the water column are <u>pelagic</u>. Among this second group are the <u>plankton</u> that cannot swim against ocean currents and the <u>nekton</u> that can swim against current flow.

20. The two zones that divide the areas of the pelagic water column are the <u>neritic zone</u> which is the area over the continental shelf, and the <u>oceanic zone</u> which represents the other pelagic areas of the ocean.

ANSWERS TO THE SUMMARY OF MODULE #9

1. The <u>intertidal</u> zone is the area of shoreline between high and low tides. It is a relatively small zone but has the greatest variation of <u>environmental factors</u> as compared to any other marine system.

2. The bottom surface, or <u>substrate</u>, of a marine habitat determines what organisms can live there. The two basic types of substrate are <u>rocky</u> and <u>sandy/muddy</u>. Animals that hold on to the surface of a substrate are called <u>epifauna</u>. They either crawl about the sea bottom or sit firmly attached to it. When such an organism is attached to a substrate, it is called <u>sessile</u>.

3. Most organisms living in the upper areas of the intertidal zone face becoming dried out, or <u>desiccated</u>, during low tide. Often they move to small areas of trapped water called <u>tidepools</u>. Stationary animals, such as barnacles and oysters, <u>seal in moisture</u>, in order to keep from drying out.

4. To avoid heating up during low tide exposure to the sun, barnacles and limpets store water to allow for <u>evaporation</u>, which cools their bodies.

5. Besides moisture level, two abiotic factors that can drastically change during low tide are <u>temperature</u> and <u>salinity</u>.

6. Most intertidal organisms are filter feeders and feed and reproduce during <u>high tide</u>. Because most organisms in this area do not move around, they produce <u>planktonic</u> gametes.

7. Waves do not usually approach the shore parallel to it but rather at an <u>angle</u>. When the closest part of the wave enters shallow water it <u>slows down</u>. This causes the wave to bend, or <u>refract</u>.

8. Most coastlines are not straight. When an area juts out farther than the rest of the coast it is a <u>headland</u>. This area experiences <u>greater</u> wave action than the surrounding areas. A <u>bay</u> is an area of coast behind the rest of the shoreline. It experiences <u>less</u> wave action.

9. On the ocean bottom, sudden depressions, called <u>canyons</u>, cause waves to bend so that shore line wave action is <u>lessened</u>. <u>Sand bars</u> and <u>reefs</u> cause the waves to break before they reach the shore.

10. Mussels avoid getting washed away from strong wave action by attaching themselves to a hard surface with strong, elastic <u>byssal threads</u>. Though waves cause potentially difficult conditions for intertidal organisms, they bring in beneficial <u>nutrient-rich water</u> and remove <u>waste</u>.

11. Fishes in the intertidal rarely have <u>swim bladders</u> because to survive in this ecosystem, they have to live on the bottom to cling to the substrate.

12. One of the most important resources in an intertidal community is <u>land</u>. Organisms create open spaces by <u>predation</u>, <u>overgrowing slower or weaker individuals</u>, or growing <u>sideways</u>, pushing other organisms out of the way. Abiotic factors that create space include <u>heavy surf</u>, <u>winter ice floes</u>, and <u>drifting debris</u>.

13. Noticeable horizontal bands of organisms living within a certain range in the intertidal zone are known as <u>vertical zonation</u>. Organisms live in these bands because of various factors. The upper limit in which an organism can live is usually determined by <u>abiotic factors</u>, such as too much sunlight, while the lower limit is usually a result of <u>biotic factors</u>, such as predation.

14. The three major zones of organisms within the rocky intertidal are the <u>upper</u>, <u>middle</u>, and <u>lower</u> zones. The highest zone is rarely submerged, extending from the highest spring tide mark to the <u>extent of water spray caused by the waves</u>. The limiting factor here, then, is <u>water</u>. Only a few gastropods and crustaceans can survive here, the most prominent being marine snails of the genus *Littorina*. The middle zone of the intertidal has such fluctuations in <u>tidal patterns</u> (such as from neap tides), there are smaller divisions of vertical zones within this area. The highest area most notably contains <u>barnacles</u>. The middle area of this center zone is dominated by aggressive <u>mussels</u>. They crowd out other organisms or simply grow over the top of them to secure the most limiting factor in this area: <u>space</u>. The lower levels of the middle intertidal zone commonly contain species of <u>algae</u> which are <u>indicator species</u>, signaling the lower limits of this area.

15. When a specific area becomes available for occupation, the process of the habitation of that area is called <u>ecological sucession</u>. When dominant species finally move into an area and become established for an extended period, that area is called a <u>climax community</u>.

16. For the greatest diversity in an area, there needs to be regular <u>disturbances</u> to keep the dominant organisms from taking over, but they cannot occur so often that the community does not have time for organisms to move in.

17. The limiting resources of the lower intertidal zone are <u>space</u> and <u>light</u>. This zone is under water most of the time and has the <u>greatest</u> diversity of intertidal organisms.

18. Soft-bottom ecosystems have <u>loose</u> sediments so organisms can burrow into them. Animals that live under the sediment of an ecosystem are called <u>infauna</u>. <u>Larger</u> types of sediments are moved around less by wave action than <u>smaller</u> types of sediments. The three general classes of sediments from smallest to largest are <u>clay</u>, <u>silt</u>, and <u>sand</u>. A combination of the two smaller types makes <u>mud</u>. Lighter, finer particles of sediment remain suspended in water much <u>longer</u> than coarser, heavier particles. The sediment of the intertidal is determined by the amount of <u>wave action</u> through the area. Calmer areas usually have bottoms made up of <u>finer</u> material. Areas with more wave action or stronger currents have a substrate of <u>coarser</u> material.

19. Detritus is found in areas with <u>finer sediments</u>, where currents are not as strong. Because water does not move as freely through fine sediments, these areas have less <u>oxygen</u> than sandy areas. As a result, the deep areas of the muddy intertidal have black layers of material that come from the <u>decomposition</u> of organic material produced under <u>anaerobic</u> conditions.

20. Most animals living in muddy substrates have to live near the substrate's <u>surface</u> and pump oxygen rich water into their bodies.

21. There are relatively few <u>primary</u> producers in a soft-bottomed ecosystem. Zonation is present in soft-bottomed ecosystems but it is more pronounced in areas with a <u>sandy</u> substrate. Sand fleas and burrowing crabs are found toward the <u>upper areas</u>. The center areas contain <u>worms and clams</u> that live under the substrate. At <u>low tide</u> level, the diversity of species <u>increases</u> and includes sand dollars and sea cucumbers.

ANSWERS TO THE SUMMARY OF MODULE #10

1. An <u>estuary</u> is a semi-enclosed area at the mouth of a river where fresh water and seawater meet and mix to create a complex ecosystem. <u>The melting of large masses of ice after an ice age</u> caused worldwide ocean levels to rise, resulting in the formation of the most common type of estuaries.

2. Evidences for an ice age include <u>glacial deposits</u>, large <u>boulders</u> that were clearly transported to their current locations, and <u>geological features</u> such as deep lakes that are best described by the action of glaciers.

3. In order for an ice age to occur, several conditions must exist. There needs to be a lot of <u>snowfall</u> and not very much <u>snow melting</u>. This means that the summers have to be <u>cooler</u>. There needs to be a greater rate of <u>evaporation of moisture</u> into the air so that water can turn into snow. This means that the ocean temperatures had to be <u>warmer</u> than they are today. Also, there needs to be extreme <u>weather patterns</u> for the extra evaporated moisture to be transported from the oceans over to the continents.

4. There are two major views when explaining the cause of an ice age. The <u>uniformitarian</u> thinks that several ice ages occurred throughout earth's history and that they all came and ended rather slowly. The <u>catastrophist</u> thinks that there was only one ice age, and it came about very quickly.

5. The five types of estuaries are: <u>drowned river valleys</u> (once narrow and deep but became broad and shallow as water levels rose), <u>bar-built estuaries</u> (formed because of a protective sand bar or barrier island blocking the fresh water coming out of the river), <u>fjords</u> (the result of glaciers cutting deeply into the earth creating a valley as they moved near the coast), <u>river deltas</u> (resulting from river water carrying eroded sediments and depositing them along the coast near the sea), and <u>tectonic estuaries</u> (formed as a result of motion in the earth's crust).

7. Salinity in an estuary varies due to <u>location</u> upstream or downstream and <u>tidal changes</u>. Because seawater is much <u>denser</u> than fresh water, it will stay on the bottom, allowing the fresh water to flow over it. This results in a <u>salt wedge</u> that moves along the estuary with the tides. In times of <u>heavy</u> river flow, the estuary will be <u>lower</u> in salinity than during times of light river flow.

8. Because of the large <u>gyres</u> in the ocean, salinity is different on different sides of an estuary's river. When you are in the ocean facing the river mouth, the low-salinity side of the river will be on your right if you are in the <u>Northern</u> Hemisphere and on your left if you are in the <u>Southern</u> Hemisphere.

9. Because river water carries fine, eroded sediments a further distance than coarse, eroded sediments, the substrate of most estuaries is composed of <u>mud</u> and fine particles. This means that these estuary sediments also contain <u>organic material</u>, which is about the same size as silt and clay. These sediments will not allow much water to flow through them and therefore do not contain a lot of <u>oxygen</u>.

10. <u>Euryhaline</u> species are very tolerant to salinity changes and can live in all parts of an estuary. <u>Stenohaline</u> species can tolerate only a narrow range of salinity changes and live on the outer edges of an estuary. <u>Brackish</u> species are those that live in water that is saltier than fresh water but not as salty as seawater. These species are found in the center area of the estuary.

11. Estuaries can be divided into three major habitats. The areas with a high elevation are called <u>wetlands</u> and are covered with water only at high tide. <u>Mudflats</u> are lower in elevation than wetlands and are regularly exposed to air and then covered by water again. <u>Channels</u> are always under water.

12. Temperate wetlands are in cooler climates of the world and contain wet, grassy areas called salt marshes. Tropical wetlands are in warmer climates and are called mangrove forests.

13. Red mangroves are able to grow directly in salt water, sending their aerial prop roots down to encourage outward growth. Black mangroves are less tolerant of salt water and grow further inland. They have a series of pencil-thin root extensions, called pneumatophores, that grow up out of the soil to allow for more oxygen exposure. Of the three mangrove types, white mangroves are the least tolerant of salt water and grow on the uppermost edge of the mangrove forest. They get rid of excess salt by excreting it through two salt glands located at the base of the leaves.

14. Since there are few land plants or algae in mudflats, diatoms and other photosynthetic plankton are the major primary producers. Some mudflat bottoms have large areas of seagrasses. Eel grass is most common in temperate areas and turtle grass is found in tropical waters. Besides contributing to primary production, grasses provide shelter for other organisms and help to hold the sediment together.

15. Bacteria thrive in the anaerobic conditions located a few inches below the surface of mudflats. They decompose organic matter. These creatures play a major role in transforming dead estuarine organisms into small food particles available to be eaten by other mudflat animals.

16. Most of the large creatures living in mudflats are infauna. The most prevalent species are several types of clams. Within this group, those with the feeding strategy of eating the detritus that has settled onto the sediment are called deposit feeders. This is the most common type of feeding strategy in this habitat. The other feeding strategy in this area is filter feeding but it is much less common.

17. Microscopic organisms living in between marine sediment particles are called meiofauna.

18. Fishes and birds are the most prominent predators in the mudflat community. Fishes enter the area at high tide, gaining access to organisms they cannot reach when the tides are low. Bird predation most often occurs at low tide, because they have access to the exposed substrate.

19. There is an interesting correlation between the length of a bird's bill and the type of organisms it eats. Those with short bills prey on organisms buried just below the surface, while those with long bills prey on organisms buried deeper. This avoids competition between different species of birds.

20. Estuarine areas where water is always present are called channels. Many fishes use these areas for spawning or as nurseries because of the abundant food and safety from predators.

21. An estuary is a very productive ecosystem. Although there are relatively few types of species present, the great quantities of organisms have a large impact on their environment. These areas are very productive because there are plenty of nutrients which are brought in from the ocean tides and river current. This supports large populations of primary producers. The excess food in the form of detritus flows out to the ocean, via a process called outwelling, to be distributed and used by surrounding ecosystems.

ANSWERS TO THE SUMMARY OF MODULE #11

1. Coral reef communities are found in the tropical zones of the earth, most occurring between the Tropic of Cancer and the Tropic of Capricorn. However, the western coasts of Central America, South America, and Africa experience a strong upwelling of cold water from the poles, which hampers coral growth in these otherwise tropical latitudes.

2. The three things that corals need in order to live are warm water, a hard substrate, and sunlight. The two major producers of coral reefs are coral animals (that make calcium carbonate armor) and coralline algae (that encrust the reef with a hard protective layer, trapping soft sediments and rubble). Corals belong to the phylum Cnidaria, class Anthozoa. The stony, or reef-building, corals are in the subclass Zoantharia.

3. Corals asexually reproduce upwards by moving up and secreting an elevated bottom and extended sides of the corallite. Coral can also asexually reproduce laterally by budding off a portion of the body and secreting a new corallite. When polyps bud sideways, a thin layer of living tissue, called a coenosarc, exists between the coral polyps. A new coral colony can also begin when a piece of existing live coral is broken off. Corals have been observed sexually reproducing by mass spawning. This is a possible benefit to corals because the large quantity of gametes provides more opportunity for survival from predators and the seasonal currents may be more beneficial to planktonic larvae.

4. Corals have a large variety of growth forms based upon their budding patterns. When coral polyps reproduce mostly vertically, the resulting formation is a branching coral. When polyps reproduce mostly horizontally, the result is encrusting or boulder corals. When there are nearly equal directions of reproduction, the coral is often foliacious.

5. Besides receiving nutrients from zooxanthellae, corals capture zooplankton for food. The three ways they do this is by using their tentacles to capture food and moving it to their centrally located mouths, secreting mucus to trap food and moving it to their mouths via the motion of cilia located on the corals' bodies, and by extending filaments out of their gut cavities to digest food particles directly. Corals use mucus and the motion of cilia to remove trapped sediments that have settled on their bodies.

6. A fringing reef is a type of coral reef that forms as a border along the coast. The three regions of this type of reef are the reef flat (located closest to shore where the water is shallow and often exposed at low tide), the reef crest (where the fringing reef begins to slope downward), and the reef slope (which slants down into deeper water).

7. A barrier reef is a coral reef that occurs away from the coast. It is separated from the shoreline by a calm lagoon. As the coral rises toward the reef flat, a back reef slope results. Sand often builds up enough to form small islands called cays or keys. The fore reef slope often experiences strong wave action and can have alternating reef projections and channels called a spur and groove formation.

8. An atoll is a ring of coral reef with steep outer slopes that enclose a shallow lagoon. It is believed that these reefs result from stages of reef building around a volcanic mountain. First, a fringing reef forms on the shallow areas surrounding the volcano. Growth continues on the outer edge of the reef because of the current and the plankton supply. After a while, a barrier reef results as the most prolific area of the reef moves more and more offshore. Over time the inactive volcano begins to sink and/or ocean levels rise until eventually a ring of coral reef is left, resulting in an atoll.

9. The fore reef slope of an atoll is located <u>outside</u> of the coral ring and is extremely steep. The back reef slope is located <u>inside</u> the ring and gently slopes downward to the inner <u>lagoon</u>. This shallow area is often interrupted by pillars of coral growth called <u>pinnacles</u> which often penetrate the ocean surface, forming islands. The side of the atoll that faces the wind is called the <u>windward</u> side and exhibits spur and groove formations. It contains coralline algae which can endure the constant plummeting of the waves, often forming an <u>algal ridge</u>. The sheltered side of an atoll is the <u>leeward</u> side.

10. Corals need to live in relatively <u>clear</u> water, but this type of water contains few <u>nutrients</u>. Despite this lack, a reef system efficiently <u>recycles</u> its nutrients and produces its own fixed <u>nitrogen</u>.

11. Corals can be fierce competitors for reef space. Some will extend <u>tiny filaments</u> out of their gut to digest their neighbor. Others have stinging <u>tentacles</u> that can injure adjacent colonies. Some are able to <u>grow</u> rapidly enough to branch out above the neighboring coral and take over its sunlight. Seaweeds do not overgrow a reef area because of the <u>nutrient-poor</u> water and the constant <u>grazing</u> of reef fishes.

12. Soft corals do not produce a <u>hard calcium carbonate exoskeleton</u> but have internal limestone spines called <u>spicules</u> that provide support and protection. They grow faster than stony corals but do not take over a coral reef most likely because they are more susceptible to <u>the strong wave action and occasional bad weather</u>. They also do not have the three sources of <u>food</u> that stony corals have.

13. There are many <u>mutualistic</u> associations between reef organisms. This makes the coral reef a more efficient habitat because it <u>provides living spaces for more organisms</u> when they are sharing locations. It also makes the best use of resources, such as <u>recycling</u> wastes or making organisms healthier. Some examples of mutualistic associations include: <u>coral</u> and zooxanthellae, remoras and sharks, <u>clownfish</u> and sea anemones, cleaner shrimp and <u>fishes</u>, and various animals <u>protecting</u> coral from crown-of-thorns sea stars.

Identification.

a. <u>tentacles</u> b. <u>mouth</u> c. <u>septa</u> d. <u>columella</u> e. <u>nematocysts</u> f. <u>coenosarc</u> g. <u>gut cavity</u> h. <u>corallite</u>

ANSWERS TO THE SUMMARY OF MODULE #12

1. The continental shelf is a gently sloping area, beginning from the low-tide mark and continuing to the shelf break. Compared to the rest of the ocean, this area is shallow. Shelves located in warmer areas of the world have <u>more</u> species of organisms living there than those located in colder areas of the world.

2. Those organisms that dwell on the bottom surface of the sea are called the <u>benthos</u>. Those organisms living up in the water column that can swim more strongly than the ocean current are called <u>nekton</u>.

3. Continental shelf areas are <u>subtidal</u>, which means that they stay underwater regardless of the tides. The <u>current</u> and <u>wave</u> action keep the water above the shelf well mixed which keeps temperature and salinity relatively constant and distributes nutrients well.

4. Heavy wave action in shelf areas washes away <u>fine particles</u> and leaves mainly a <u>sandy</u> substrate, while areas with little wave action, or those that are protected from it, have <u>fine</u> sediments.

5. Continental shelf communities can be divided into two groups based on the ocean floor substrate. They are <u>soft-bottom shelf</u> communities and <u>hard-bottom shelf</u> communities. There are three types of benthic organisms that live in these areas: <u>infauna</u> (which live buried in the sediment), <u>epifauna</u> (which live on the surface of the sediment), and <u>meiofauna</u> (which live in between the sediment particles).

6. In contrast to soft-bottom estuaries, soft-bottom subtidal communities have a <u>larger</u> number of species living in them because the <u>physical</u> conditions do not change as drastically as in estuaries. Soft-bottom subtidal communities can have muddy bottoms or sandy bottoms. The <u>muddy</u> bottoms have a buildup of organic material because there is little water flow through the substrate and as a result, less <u>oxygen</u>. Because of this, most infauna have to live buried <u>just below the surface</u>. In sandy substrates, where there is <u>less</u> organic buildup and <u>more</u> oxygen, infauna will be buried much <u>deeper</u>.

7. The infauna are <u>not evenly</u> spaced in the substrate of soft bottom shelf communities. Scientists do not yet understand why, but they tend to live in <u>patches or clumps</u>. Scientists have been able to better study these areas since the invention of scuba, an acronym for <u>self-contained underwater breathing apparatus</u>.

8. Soft-bottom shelf environments are further divided into two types: <u>unvegetated</u> (where there is little vegetation), and <u>vegetated</u> (where there is plenty of vegetation). In areas with little vegetation, <u>detritus</u>, coming from nearby estuaries and other shore communities, is a key food source.

9. <u>Meiofauna</u> are microscopic creatures that make their home in the spaces in between the individual particles of <u>sediment</u>, either attaching directly to the particles or moving in between them.

10. In soft-bottom shelf communities, <u>substrate</u> type determines the major feeding strategies among organisms living there. <u>Deposit</u> feeders are more common in muddy bottoms because of the presence of more detritus. <u>Suspension</u> feeders are more predominant in sandy bottoms because there is a greater amount of water flow through the substrate, bringing in suspended food. These two types of feeding strategies are not commonly found close together because <u>deposit</u> feeders churn through sediments, stirring them up. This can clog the filtering mechanisms of the <u>suspension</u> feeders.

11. Among the vegetated soft-bottom environments, turtle grass is most commonly found growing in the tropics, while eelgrass is more commonly found in temperate areas. Seagrass roots can remove more nutrients from the sediments than algae, resulting in better nutrient flow in this type of ecosystem versus an unvegetated ecosystem. Seagrasses not only carry out the majority of primary production in these areas, but their blades are locations on which both algae and other organisms directly dwell. Their roots also aid in keeping the soft substrate more stable. Most organisms feed on decaying seagrasses instead of live seagrasses.

12. Hard-bottom subtidal communities are usually densely covered with seaweeds because there is a hard substrate on which to attach. Sessile animals, such as sea urchins, crabs, and snails live here, too. Epifauna dominate the hard-bottom areas because there is little soft substrate into which infauna can burrow.

13. Many seaweeds are able to utilize the same space by time-sharing. There are also several strategies employed by many seaweed species to keep from being eaten. Some species have special chemicals that give them a bad flavor, some are leather-like and difficult to eat, and others incorporate calcium carbonate into their tissues to give them a hard outer surface.

14. When kelps are not tall enough to form a surface canopy, the community they form is referred to as a kelp bed. When the kelps are tall enough to reach the surface and form a canopy, the community is a kelp forest. Kelps need sunlight, a hard substrate on which to attach, and cold nutrient rich water in order to grow.

15. Kelps exhibit an alternation of generations life cycle. The large thallus forming forests and beds is the sporophyte generation. It is a diploid generation, undergoing meiosis and producing haploid spores. When the spores germinate, they grow into the gametophyte generation, the generation that is haploid and produces gametes. In kelps, this generation is usually very small and often microscopic.

16. The kelp forest canopy often shades light from the bottom surface. The resulting habitat layers are made up of kelp species based upon their heights and the depth at which they grow. Among the animals that live in this understory, small sessile organisms live directly on the kelp blades and stipes. Between the kelp live creatures such as sponges, and octopuses. Fishes inhabit all levels of the kelp forest.

17. The broken pieces of floating kelp, often called drift kelp, result from wave action. They often sink to the bottom and are eaten, primarily by sea urchins. When there is not enough of this food available, sea urchins will often feed directly on the holdfasts of living kelp, causing the seaweed to float to the surface and eventually die.

ANSWERS TO THE SUMMARY OF MODULE #13

1. The <u>epipelagic</u> zone extends from the surface of the water down to about 200m. It overlaps with the photic zone, which varies in depth based on <u>light penetration</u>. Water in this zone located over the continental shelf is called <u>neritic</u>, while water lying over the rest of the ocean is referred to as <u>oceanic</u>.

2. Though photosynthesis can occur in much of the epipelagic zone, there is no input of <u>nutrients</u> from other ecosystems. Virtually all of the food is <u>self-produced</u>. Because of a large population of phytoplankton, there are enough nutrients produced for <u>organisms in this zone</u> and <u>other zones</u> as well.

3. Nutrients from the epipelagic reaches zones below it two main ways. Living creatures can <u>swim down to a deeper zone and be eaten there</u>. Also, unused organic material can <u>sink into a lower zone</u>.

4. From smallest to largest, the four main plankton groups are <u>picoplankton</u>, <u>ultraplankton</u>, <u>nanoplankton</u>, and <u>microplankton</u>. Diatoms and dinoflagellates are a part of <u>microplankton</u>. The most abundant crustacean members of the epipelagic microplankton are the <u>copepods</u>. The smallest bacteria and cyanobacteria are a part of the <u>picoplankton</u>. Most of the organisms in the smaller three groups are not limited to one climate and therefore are present in <u>greater</u> quantities in the ocean than diatoms and dinoflagellates. It is believed that these small phytoplankton account for most of the <u>primary production</u> in the ocean.

5. <u>Cyanobacteria</u> can survive in nutrient-poor waters because they are nitrogen fixers. <u>Coccolithophores</u>, members of the nanoplankton, are armored with calcareous plates that are thought to reflect the intense light of the tropics.

6. <u>Larvaceans</u> use their mucus coverings to trap members of the nano-, ultra-, and picoplankton. When the filters in their mucus "nets" get clogged, the creatures <u>shed them and create new ones</u>. Once that happens, they become a <u>plentiful food source</u> for other animals in the ocean. <u>Pteropods</u> are small, snail-like mollusks that have a foot that resembles a pair of wings. These are used to <u>keep the animal suspended in the water</u>.

7. Zooplankton can be divided into two groups: <u>holoplankton</u> (which spend their entire lives as plankton), and <u>meroplankton</u> (which spend only part of their lives as plankton).

8. As a general rule, most species of organisms among the epipelagic nekton are <u>carnivorous predators</u>. <u>Planktivorous</u> creatures are those that only feed only on plankton. Some of these predators are quite small, such as <u>sardines and anchovies</u>, while others are quite large, such as <u>baleen whales and whale sharks</u>.

9. There are two major strategies to staying suspended in the epipelagic zone. An organism can have <u>physical features that create drag</u>, or an organism can employ <u>buoyancy</u>. An object's <u>shape</u> affects the speed at which it sinks in the water. When water resists the motion of objects, it is called <u>drag</u>. The more <u>surface area</u> on an organism, the higher its resistance in the water. <u>A flattened shape</u>, <u>long spines</u>, and/or <u>feathery projections</u> are ways to create more resistance.

10. Nektonic organisms need to be <u>streamlined</u> in order to swim well. To help stay afloat, they have to create <u>buoyancy</u>. An organism can do this by storing <u>oils or fats</u> in the body or by utilizing <u>gases</u> for flotation. Many fishes have a <u>swim bladder</u>, for example, that is filled with gases that can expand or contract as the animals move up or down in the water column.

11. Some plankton, called <u>neuston</u>, live right on the surface of the water. Most of them, such as the Portuguese man-of-war and the by-the-wind sailor have a <u>gas-filled structure</u> that helps them float.

12. Since there are no objects to hide behind, the best way to hide in the epipelagic is to use <u>special coloration for camouflage</u> or to be <u>as transparent as possible</u>. Most fishes in this zone display <u>countershading</u>, where their dorsal surface is darkly colored and their ventral surface is silvery white.

13. Epipelagic fishes are usually shaped with slightly <u>laterally</u> flattened bodies with few projections, <u>small</u> scales (or none at all), and <u>stiff, narrow</u> fins that behave like rudders for steering.

14. Many epipelagic fishes have a large amount of a protein called <u>myoglobin</u> in their blood. This provides more <u>oxygen</u> availability for better muscle movement. Their interior protein-rich layer of dark muscle is also <u>warmer</u> and allows for longer swimming duration due to a <u>better environment in which the muscles can work</u>. Epipelagic fishes, then, use their dark inner muscles to provide long-duration swimming, and they use their light outer muscles for <u>sudden bursts of speed</u>.

15. Many epipelagic zooplankton undergo <u>vertical migration</u>, diving down to great depths during the day in order to avoid predation, and returning at night to feed.

16. <u>Dissolved organic matter</u> (DOM) is organic material that is dissolved in the ocean water, coming directly out of the cells of phytoplankton or produced as a result of waste products from protozoans. DOM is part of the <u>microbial loop</u>, which is a flow of energy moving throughout the plankton. The DOM is eaten by <u>bacteria</u> which are eaten by <u>protozoans</u>, which are eaten by <u>zooplankton</u>, finally making the energy bound up in the DOM available to the rest of the food chain. Organic matter that is not dissolved, such as fecal pellets and discarded larvacean mucus containers, is called <u>detritus</u>.

17. Not all ocean surfaces have the same production rates due to different intensities of light. Light availability in the epipelagic is affected by <u>latitude</u>, <u>sediments</u>, <u>weather and seasons</u>, and <u>plankton concentration</u>. When looking at global primary production, there are higher rates of production in <u>coastal</u> areas (from regular nutrient mixing due to wind and waves), <u>warmer</u> areas (from year-round light availability), <u>equatorial</u> areas (from equatorial upwelling and plentiful sunlight), and <u>extreme polar</u> areas (from overturn and winter mixing).

18. As a rule, overturn occurs at the <u>polar latitudes</u> during the winter. Because of low light levels in the winter, however, primary production is not boosted by this until <u>spring</u>. Primary production is low in the center of the <u>gyres</u> because these areas are located in fairly warm latitudes where the surface waters will not cool enough for overturn or surface mixing.

19. <u>El Niño</u> is the term describing a change in the surface currents on the Peruvian and Chilean coasts of South America. The winds and resulting upwelling are <u>decreased</u>, reducing the number of fish caught by fishermen. Every couple of years, this phenomenon is more drastic. In India, a phenomenon called <u>southern oscillation</u> results in strong summer monsoons alternating with weaker summer monsoon seasons. Both of these phenomena are related via see-saw like changes in <u>barometric pressure</u>. The combined situation is called <u>ENSO</u>.

ANSWERS TO THE SUMMARY OF MODULE #14

1. The mesopelagic zone is the pelagic layer of the ocean where light can penetrate, but not enough to support photosynthesis. There is enough light for creatures to see one another, so many of them have light-producing structures called photophores. The temperature division called the thermocline is in this zone.

2. Though there are some exceptions, most are relatively small compared to the organisms in the epipelagic. This is because, with no photosynthesis, this zone depends on excess primary production from other zones, meaning there is little food available to support large organisms. Since there is not enough light for photosynthesis, phytoplankton cannot survive here, although zooplankton can.

3. As the ocean depth increases, the quantity of organisms decreases because there is less and less food available to support organisms.

4. The two most common fishes in the mesopelagic zone are bristlemouths and lanternfishes. Ostracods, or "seed shrimp," are interesting crustaceans that live in this zone as well.

5. Because food is relatively scarce, it is helpful for organisms in this zone to have mechanisms to capture as much prey as possible. Many have broad feeding habits, eating nearly anything that comes into their path. Some have a sit-and-wait strategy, with body features like very little muscle, watery flesh, and no swim bladder because they do not have to chase down prey. Many are neutrally buoyant, meaning that they do not have to expend energy to remain in one spot.

6. A second feeding strategy in this zone is vertical migration, where organisms swim up to the shallow waters to feed at night and move back down to the depths in the day. These fishes have large muscles, strong bones, and a swim bladder for buoyancy. They can also tolerate drastic changes in temperature and pressure as they migrate.

7. Fishes in this zone have sensory organs such as tubular eyes and long lateral lines that follow the length of their bodies. To keep from being detected, many creatures exhibit either transparency (upper mesopelagic) or countershading (lower mesopelagic). Red light does not penetrate water as deeply as blue light and therefore cannot be seen in great depths.

8. Another successful strategy to hide is to use bioluminescence (the production of visible light). This is used to break up an organism's silhouette. It can also be used to identify members of the same species, defense, or as a means of seeing other creatures. The two biological chemicals that create this light when mixed in the presence of oxygen are luciferin (a protein) and luciferase (an enzyme). This light reaction is unique in that it is a cool reaction and will not harm living organisms. At colder temperatures, the chemical reactions that cause light run more slowly than in warmer temperatures.

9. Pressure is an important physical factor in determining where deep sea organisms can live. This factor increases with depth. The deep sea is divided into three zones based on the amount they experience: the bathypelagic zone, the abyssopelagic zone, and the hadalpelagic zone.

11. In the deep sea there is no light so organisms do not need countershading. They are generally grayish and have either small eyes or none at all. Most creatures are bioluminescent, but their photophores are not located on their ventral side like mesopelagic creatures.

12. In the deep sea, even less <u>food</u> is available than what is present in the mesopelagic. Most organisms are therefore very small and move slowly. There are no <u>vertical migrators</u> from the deep sea because the epipelagic is too far. Thus, most creatures have <u>small</u> muscles, <u>weak</u> skeletons, and no <u>swim bladders</u>. They have <u>large mouths</u> to eat whatever prey they find.

13. Many deep sea creatures have the ability to produce both eggs and sperm. The term for this is <u>hermaphroditic</u>. These individuals can mate with any other member of their species, making it easier to <u>find a mate</u>. <u>Male parasitism</u> is where the male of a species attaches to a female and draws nutrients from her. However, both individuals actually benefit – the male gets <u>nutrients</u> and the female <u>will always have a mate</u>.

15. Larvae from deep sea organisms cannot exert enough energy to travel <u>where there are large populations of plankton</u>. Instead, they develop in large <u>eggs</u> with lots of <u>yolk</u> to feed them until they can feed on bigger creatures.

16. It is difficult to study deep sea creatures because <u>they live at great depths under great pressure</u>. Scientists observe these organisms by using <u>deep water cameras</u> and <u>submersibles</u>.

17. It is easier for organisms to find food on the deep sea floor because any food that sinks past a pelagic organism is <u>forever lost to it</u>. But on the sea floor, food collects there until <u>it is found</u>. Therefore, most fishes that feed in this area have <u>large, muscular</u> bodies to presumably be able to search wide areas looking for food.

18. On the deep sea floor, <u>bacteria</u> break down the non-readily digestible skeletal remains. <u>Meiofauna</u> (the largest animal group in this area), then feed on both these organisms and the broken down material, making the nutrients available to the rest of the deep sea food chain. Overall, <u>deposit</u> feeders dominate this zone, as opposed to suspension feeders.

19. An interesting occurrence among many species of deep sea creatures is that of <u>gigantism</u>, in which an organism grows to an extreme size. This is difficult for scientists to explain because, as a general rule, deep sea organisms are smaller because <u>the scarcity of food</u> should make it hard for a large creature to survive.

20. <u>Hydrothermal</u> vents have black smokers as a result of precipitation of mineral rich vent water which includes <u>hydrogen sulfide</u>. They are also much <u>warmer</u> in temperature and are located at <u>fast spreading</u> oceanic plates. <u>Cold seeps</u> have white smokers as a result of precipitation of mineral rich vent water which includes <u>light-colored dissolved zinc sulfides</u>. They are <u>cooler</u> in temperature and are located at <u>slow spreading</u> plate areas. Both locations support deep sea <u>chemosynthetic</u> communities by bringing up chemical nutrients for <u>chemosynthetic</u> bacteria.

21. Most recently, it was discovered that, despite the lack of sunlight, <u>photosynthesis</u> *does* occur in the deep sea. This is because hydrothermal vents produce <u>blackbody radiation</u>, the emission of infrared light, which can be used for this process. The photosynthetic creatures are very efficient in their ability to collect the few emitted <u>photons of light</u>.

ANSWERS TO THE SUMMARY OF MODULE #15

1. The largest group of harvested ocean organisms is made up of species of <u>fishes</u>. In fishery terminology, members of this group are called <u>finfish</u>. The next largest group of harvested ocean creatures is <u>shellfish</u>, comprised of crustaceans and mollusks.

2. The best fishing grounds in the world are located in the <u>photic</u> zone, near the <u>coasts</u>. Fishing grounds are especially rich where there is <u>coastal upwelling</u> (which provides plentiful nutrients) and wide <u>continental shelves</u> (which provide good locations for large populations to grow).

3. Two major areas of the world that are rich with food resources are the coastlines near <u>Antarctica</u> and some areas around the <u>North Pole</u>. These resources are not extensively harvested because <u>they are remote and the harsh climate prevents it</u>.

4. <u>Clupeoid</u> fishes are small, plankton-eating fishes that travel in large schools. <u>Gadoid</u> fishes are larger, bottom-dwelling fishes. The first group is collected by <u>industrial</u> fisheries and is used for fish meal, margarine, cosmetics, paints, and pet food.

5. Small, schooling, plankton-eating fishes are most often harvested in a type of netting called a <u>purse seine</u>. Bottom dwellers are most often caught with <u>trawls</u> that catch anything that lives on the ocean bottom.

6. <u>Tuna</u> are the largest of the commercial species of fishes. They are often the top carnivores in the ocean's food webs.

7. Fisheries use <u>longlines</u>, which are made up of lengthy, floating mainlines, to capture the largest commercial fishes. Some fisheries use <u>gill nets</u>, which are designed to entangle fishes that are not small enough to fit through the net opening. A major drawback to this second method is that <u>the nets will trap any creature that cannot fit through the net opening</u>, so many fishes and marine mammals that are not intended to be captured are killed.

8. <u>Renewable</u> resources are resources that can naturally replace harvested numbers while <u>nonrenewable</u> resources are resources that are not capable of replacing harvested numbers. Yet, even if a resource can naturally replace itself, it can still be harvested to the point of <u>extinction</u>.

9. The <u>sustainable yield</u> of a population is the amount of individuals in a population that can be caught without reducing the size of the population or letting it grow. This situation often occurs when a population is not extremely large or extremely small. The <u>maximum sustainable yield</u> is the amount that can be harvested from a population that is in this medium-sized range, and it is unlikely to threaten the long-term size of a population.

10. If fishereies' catches exceed the quantity that keeps a population from being able to reproduce so that the population will not shrink, it is called <u>overfishing</u>. It results when the <u>maximum sustainable yield</u> is surpassed.

11. When fisheries practice prudent harvesting techniques, it is known as <u>fisheries mamagement</u>. Some of these techniques include harvesting a species <u>during certain times of the year</u>, regulating the <u>size</u> of individuals captured, allowing only certain methods of <u>capture</u>, and setting up <u>reserves</u> where no harvesting can occur.

14. An <u>exclusive economic zone</u> is an offshore area belonging exclusively to the geographically bordering country. That country has complete control of all of those resources located within that area.

15. Another way to manage fish populations in the ocean is to encourage a market for <u>non-traditional, readily available protein sources</u>. This can reduce the demand for a species that has a dwindling population and replace it with demand for a species that is plentiful.

16. <u>Mariculture</u> is the farming and harvesting of marine animals and plants. In a <u>closed</u> system, environmental factors are completely controlled by the farmer. However, this system limits the <u>types of species</u> possible to farm; <u>facilities and man power</u> are very expensive; organisms with <u>varying food and habitat requirements</u> during their life cycles are difficult to manage; and <u>parasites or diseases</u> may suddenly occur. It is less expensive to run an <u>open</u> system, but some drawbacks include: <u>weather, pollution</u>, and <u>changing seasons</u> that can adversely affect the organisms; the high concentration of creatures can cause <u>nutrient buildups</u> that result in harmful algal blooms; and <u>natural habitats</u> often have to be destroyed to make room for the facilities.

17. The <u>migratory</u> habits of salmon are helpful to mariculture facilities. The salmon can be hatched and raised through juvenile stages in the facility. At that point they can then be released into the river so that they can <u>migrate out to the ocean</u>. They do not have to be fed or housed during their adult stages. When they return to their place of hatching, the <u>mariculture facility can conveniently harvest them</u>.

18. There are many nonliving resources in the ocean. They include <u>oil</u>, <u>energy (in the form of waves, currents, and tides)</u>, <u>various minerals</u>, and <u>water</u>.

19. The process of taking seawater, removing its salts, and creating fresh water is called <u>desalinization</u>. Dissolved substances can be removed from ocean water by <u>distillation</u> or <u>reverse osmosis</u>. The first method's drawbacks include <u>a great amount of salty residue</u> and <u>a large energy requirement</u>. The second method involves water being moved via excessive pressure from an area of <u>high dissolved-substance</u> concentration to <u>low dissolved-substance</u> concentration.

ANSWERS TO THE SUMMARY OF MODULE #16

1. Ocean habitats can be affected by human activity. A direct effect on a habitat is a change <u>that is caused at the time of the activity</u>. An indirect effect on a habitat is when a change occurs <u>as a result of an earlier activity or when a change occurs in a different location than that of the affected area</u>.

2. Human activities not geographically located near the ocean may still affect the ocean because many materials can be carried to the ocean via <u>waterways</u>, <u>trickling down through the earth</u>, and even <u>floating in the air</u>. Runoff containing excess nutrients can cause <u>algal blooms</u> that block sunlight from reef environments or pollute the water with toxic algal by-products.

3. Corals are affected by excessive coastal construction because it can cause increased <u>erosion</u>, which puts extra sediments into the water. This limits <u>sunlight penetration</u> and smothers existing corals. Also, new coral polyps <u>cannot settle onto the soft substrate</u>, and therefore the reefs cannot grow.

4. When corals spontaneously throw off a majority of their symbiotic zooxanthellae, it is called <u>bleaching</u>, and is an indication that the coral is under stress and vulnerable to disease. When divers use <u>poisons such as cyanide</u> to stun and capture reef fish, it can either kill the nearby coral or cause it to throw off its zooxanthellae.

5. There are two types of pollution: <u>natural</u> and <u>human-made</u>. Some examples of the type that does not involve humans include <u>volcanic eruptions</u> and <u>deep ocean seeps</u>. Human activity produces <u>sewage</u> (wastewater from cities, factories, and other industries). When it is treated, it is often mixed with <u>chlorine</u> to kill harmful bacteria. The residual chemicals from this treatment can be as deadly to ocean animals as when the material is untreated.

6. When solids settle out of solution from treated sewage and are broken down by decomposing bacteria, the resulting material is called <u>sludge</u>. This material is not unlike <u>detritus</u> so it can be used as fertilizer or can be pumped into marshes where bacteria in the mud can break down the organic matter.

7. <u>Eutrophication</u> is excessive algal growth as a result of increased nutrient input. This can happen when runoff containing fertilizers and wastes, especially from <u>farming</u>, enters the ocean at high rates.

8. <u>Oil</u> is one of the most common pollutants in the ocean. Sometimes it enters the ocean through natural structures called <u>seeps</u>. Most of its components cannot dissolve in water, but <u>float on the surface</u>. In small quantities, some of the hydrocarbons evaporate and the rest are broken down by <u>bacteria</u>. Ecosystems that have <u>little wave and tidal action</u> cannot survive this type of pollution as well as ecosystems that have strong water movement.

9. Human activity can put oil into the ocean in several ways: offshore oil well <u>blowouts</u>, <u>supertanker accidents</u>, city <u>runoff</u>, underground <u>storage tank release</u>, and <u>bilge water release</u> from boats.

10. Spilled oil is harmful to marine birds because it <u>nullifies the insulation ability of a bird's feathers</u> and <u>it prevents them from flying</u>.

11. Chemicals such as DDT and PCBs are synthetic pollutants, meaning that <u>they are not naturally occurring chemicals that find their way into ecosystems</u>. Both of these chemicals are in a large class of chemicals called <u>chlorinated hydrocarbons</u>. These compounds are harmful in ecosystems because they do not naturally break down into their initial components. This means they are <u>nonbiodegradable</u>.

12. A chemical such as DDT is not digested or excreted once in an organism's body. Instead, because it is <u>fat-soluble</u>, it usually gets incorporated into an animal's fat cells and stored there. This accumulation in body tissue is called <u>bioaccumulation</u>. If a contaminated organism is eaten, the DDT in its body becomes <u>incorporated into the fats of the consumer's body</u>. As the chemicals move up the <u>trophic</u> pyramid, they get more concentrated. This phenomenon is known as <u>biomagnification.</u>

13. We know that DDT travels throughout the world because <u>it exists in virtually all parts of the biosphere</u> despite the fact that it is human made and was only used in certain areas of the world.

14. Chemicals that are <u>nonbiodegradable</u> and <u>fat soluble</u> will remain stored in the tissues of affected organisms and remain in the food web.

15. <u>Heavy metals</u>, such as mercury, are naturally occurring components of the ocean, existing in small concentrations. Discharges from manufacturing plants can result in higher concentrations, which make these elements toxic to living things. These elements can accumulate in the food chain, causing <u>top carnivores</u>, such as sharks and swordfish, to have extremely high levels in their tissue. For this reason, <u>people susceptible to illness</u>, <u>pregnant women</u>, and <u>nursing mothers</u> should not eat these fishes.

16. <u>Fouling organisms</u> are those creatures that live attached to surfaces that are under water, causing negative effects to ships. The <u>paints</u> historically used to prevent these creatures from attaching to ships contain toxic chemicals. It is important to keep these creatures off ships, however, because <u>they disintegrate ship hulls</u> and <u>add to the drag the ships experience</u>. This indirectly results in more pollution because it requires more materials to build more ships and more fuel.

17. <u>Radioactive waste</u>, a byproduct of nuclear energy, is perhaps a greater threat than many other pollutants because <u>it is potentially harmful to all life forms and does not have to be eaten to harm an organism</u>. It must be carefully disposed of in a place that is both remote and will remain stable for many years because it can remain toxic for <u>potentially millions of years</u>.

18. <u>Plastic</u> debris is potentially harmful to ocean organisms because it is nonbiodegradable and often resembles <u>food</u>, so it is eaten by marine organisms. Plastics like fishing line can <u>entangle or strangulate marine animals</u>.

19. We should care for the ocean's ecosystems but, in doing so, must keep in mind <u>the welfare of people</u>. Many people depend on the ocean for survival, and restricting their use of the ocean can cause suffering or death. Also, pollutants that foul marine ecosystems are often a result of <u>processes which save lives</u>. We have to find ways to care for marine ecosystems that do not interfere with the health of people.

20. Occasionally scientists intentionally sink <u>concrete blocks and ships</u> into the ocean. They do this to provide <u>hard substrates</u> on which new coral polyps can attach. This can then eventually become <u>the base of a new, large reef</u> that supports a thriving ecosystem.

TEST FOR MODULE #1

1. Define the following terms:

a. Oceanic crust
b. Continental crust
c. Mid-ocean ridge
d. Subduction
e. Salinity
f. Coriolis effect
g. Gyres

2. If an organism had sufficient energy (and time) and had no restrictions on its temperature, salinity or food requirements, could it conceivably travel through all four major ocean basins of the world? Why or why not?

3. Why is oceanic crust under water, while continental crust is not?

4. How is new sea floor created?

5. Why is there more life in the continental shelf region of the ocean than in the abyssal plain?

6. Name one benefit hydrogen bonding provides for marine organisms.

7. How do salinity and temperature affect the density of water?

8. Along a certain fictitious seashore, there is a processing plant that dumps its byproducts of sand and clay into the ocean. Assuming everything else is the same along this shore, would you expect more or less life near the processing plant? Why?

9. All the major currents of the ocean are driven by what phenomenon?

10. Why is the average surface temperature of the ocean near the coast of Portugal much colder than the average surface temperature of North Carolina even though they are at similar latitudes?

11. What is the difference between a spring tide and a neap tide? What causes this difference?

12. If an organism is in the deep layer of the ocean, what feature of the vertical parts of the ocean would it have to cross in order to get to the warmer surface layer above it?

TEST FOR MODULE #2

1. Define the following terms:

a. Autotrophs
b. Heterotrophs
c. Respiration
d. Homeostasis
e. Poikilotherm
f. Homeotherm
g. Binomial nomenclature

2. What are the four major groups of organic molecules involved in the metabolic process?

3. Suppose the population of marine algae in Creation increased dramatically. What would most likely happen to the levels of oxygen and carbon dioxide in the atmosphere?

4. As you will learn in a later module, there are organisms down in the very deep parts of the ocean where light cannot penetrate. These organisms, however, can produce their own energy from various chemicals in their environment. Would you classify these individuals as autotrophs or heterotrophs?

5. If a single-celled organism can propel itself through the water, can you tell if it is a prokaryote or a eukaryote just by this information?

6. Distinguish between an organ and a tissue.

7. Which part of a cell allows only selected molecules to enter inside?

8. Tide pools are areas at the shoreline of oceans that sometimes become isolated from the waves and thus are exposed to the sun's heat, evaporation, or rain. If an osmoregulator found itself in such a tide pool, would the composition of its body fluids change with the changing tide pool conditions?

9. Explain how a large tuna can remain active in cold water despite the fact that its body temperature changes with its environment.

10. Corals are organisms that can reproduce both asexually by individuals dividing into two identical individuals, or sexually by broadcasting gametes into the water. If you come across a colony of coral that is connected together, is it more likely that the individuals in this colony are a result of asexual reproduction or sexual reproduction?

11. Two marine organisms appear to be very similar and are bred together in an aquarium, producing offspring. The aquarium owner tries to breed the next generation a year later in order to sell their offspring, but they do not appear to be fertile. Assuming there is no problem with the water quality or nutrition, what could you suppose about the first two organisms?

TEST FOR MODULE #3

1. Define the following terms:

a. Bacteria
b. Decomposers
c. Phytoplankton
d. Zooplankton
e. Thallus
f. Haploid
g. Diploid
h. Symbiosis

2. What are two processes that autotrophic bacteria can use to convert energy into organic matter?

3. Why aren't cyanobacteria considered algae?

4. List two ways diatoms benefit humans.

5. While hiking, you find a large amount of abrasive, whitish powder on the side of a mountain. Your guide says it is made up of tiny fossilized bits of silica. How do you know that this area was probably once under the ocean?

6. Why won't some restaurants serve fish harvested in areas of planktonic blooms?

7. What is the function of the pneumatocysts on a thallus?

8. Which type of algae (green, brown, or red) provides merchants with the emulsifying agent called algin? What does algin do?

9. A seaweed that follows the alternation of generations life cycle produces haploid (1n) spores. Into what type of generation will those haploid spores develop: sporophyte or gametophyte? Will that new generation be haploid or diploid?

10. What two types of organisms are associated with one another in a lichen?

11. Why don't the seagrasses need large, showy flowers?

12. What part of the red mangrove can help to accumulate sediment buildup?

TEST FOR MODULE #4

1. Define the following terms:

a. Amoebocytes
b. Metamorphosis
c. Polyp
d. Medusa

e. Mesoglea
f. Mutualism
g. Commensalism
h. Parasitism

2. Give one example each of a marine organism that exhibits (1) radial symmetry and (2) bilateral symmetry.

3. What are the two possible forms of support in sponges?

4. Despite the fact that polyps are generally stationary, cnidarians with only a polyp form can spread to populate vast regions of the ocean. How do they accomplish this without moving?

5. Give at least three features common to cnidarians in both the polyp and medusa stages.

6. Which of the three classes of phylum Cnidaria is composed of organisms spending most, if not all, of their life cycle as a large medusa form: the Hydrozoa, the Scyphozoa, or the Anthozoa?

7. A coral reef is a colony of anthozoan polyps. What part of it is actually alive?

8. An organism has a brain. Is it most likely bilaterally symmetric or radially symmetric?

9. A worm has no gut. Of the worms we studied in this module, which kind is it?

10. Give an example of a parasite from this module.

11. An organism is described as having a definite head and rear end; its long, thin body is made up of a series of similar compartments; and it has a definite, fluid-filled coelom. In what phylum would you classify this animal?

12. The lophophorates are grouped together because all the organisms have a lophophore. What is this structure, and what does it do?

TEST FOR MODULE #5

1. Define the following terms:

a. Mantle   e. Cephalothorax
b. Radula   f. Carapace
c. Chitin   g. Ambulacral groove
d. Molting   h. Dorsal nerve cord

2. The organisms in the phylum Mollusca have a diverse array of body forms. What are two basic body parts that most members of this group have in common?

3. Give an example of a gastropod, an example of a bivalve, and an example of a cephalopod.

4. Identify the structures in the clam illustration below:

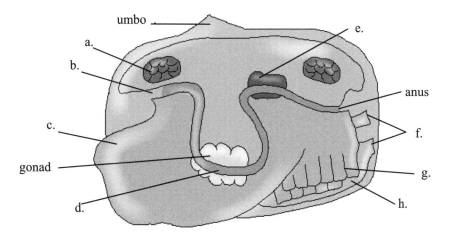

5. In an aquarium, you find what appears to be a shrimp sitting among the plants and rocks, yet when you reach in to pick it up, you find that it is just an outer covering that is completely hollow. What must have happened?

6. Cleaner shrimp display the symbiosis of mutualism in the ocean. Explain this relationship and with what organisms the shrimp are involved.

7. Explain how most female crustaceans can hatch multiple batches of fertilized eggs even though they may not be near males often.

8. What is the importance of the water vascular system in the echinoderms?

9. At a marine aquarium tide pool tank, some children are taking turns holding a sea cucumber. They begin to play with it rather roughly, and suddenly a large amount of material is squirted out of the sea cucumber's body. What happened? Is the sea cucumber hurt?

10. Explain why sea cucumbers and sea urchins need long, coiled guts.

11. A biologist is examining some recently collected marine water under a microscope and notices some echinoderm gametes. She reasons that she had better study them closely now, because it will probably be a while before water from the same region will once again contain such gametes. Why is her reasoning likely to be correct?

12. What is the function of a notochord? Adult tunicates do not have a notochord. What feature performs the notochord's function in the adults?

13. Give two examples of organisms that are in phylum Chordata but are invertebrates.

14. In which phylum do you find each of the following and what is its function?

      a. radula   b. exoskeleton   c. water vascular system   d. notochord

TEST FOR MODULE #6

1. Define the following terms:

a. Demersal
b. Chromatophores
c. Hermaphroditism
d. Oviparous
e. Viviparous

2. The members of class Agnatha are characterized by features they do not have. Name two of those features.

3. Some birds and marine mammals are considered by scientists to be very "advanced" because of their remarkable ability to migrate from one area of the world to the other without ever having been shown the way. How could you refute this statement using the lampreys as an example?

4. A fish has a jaw, but its skeleton contains no osteocytes or osteoblasts. Is it a lamprey, a ray, or a bony fish?

5. The design of rays is perfect for their demersal life style. Name two characteristics helpful to these fish.

6. What *external* feature on a bony fish ensures that the water flows across the gills so as to maximize the amount of oxygen that gets into the capillaries of the gills?

7. What special feature does a bony fish have that aids in its ability to rise in the water column?

8. Name at least three physical features of a bony fish that distinguish it from a cartilaginous fish.

9. A fish has a large, dark spot near its tail. Is this an example of camouflage, disguise, or advertisement?

10. Explain the purpose of the spiral intestine in sharks.

11. What is the name for the specialized system of blood flow in the gills of fishes?

12. What are the lateral line and ampullae of Lorenzini in sharks?

13. Explain the difference between anadromous behavior and catadromous behavior in fishes.

14. A certain fish produces only a few eggs for fertilization. Is this fish most likely oviparous or ovoviviparous?

(The test is continued on the next page.)

15. Identify the structures pointed out in the diagram below:

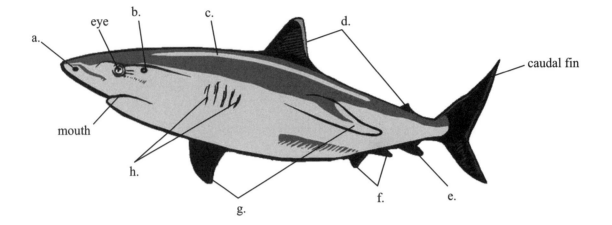

TEST FOR MODULE #7

1. Define the following terms:

a. Adaptation
b. Baleen
c. Echolocation
d. Behavior
e. Delayed implantation

2. During the time of year when sea turtle eggs hatch, the population of predatory birds near the shoreline tends to increase. Why?

3. What does the salt gland do for marine birds?

4. How is the adaptation of a laterally flattened tail helpful to marine iguanas and sea snakes?

5. Where are you more likely to find marine reptiles: warmer or colder climates?

6. Pelicans and terns both dive into the water to catch their prey. Pelicans are better swimmers, however. Why?

7. A person finds a very large jawbone washed up on the beach. It is so large that it must be from a whale. How can the person tell if it was from a baleen whale or not?

8. The largest animals on earth, the baleen whales, feed on the tiniest of organisms, the plankton. How can a diet of such small organisms be beneficial to support such huge organisms?

9. Which marine mammal order contains animals that spend their entire lives in the water: Sirenia, Pinnipedia, or Carnivora?

10. Would you expect to find a melon on a toothed whale or a baleen whale?

11. Consider the echolocation system of a dolphin. Explain how the clicks are generated in the dolphin, as well as how the echoes are received and processed. Include the major anatomical structures related to the echolocation system in your answer.

12. Why do dolphins not get the bends when they dive deeply?

13. You see what might be a seal or a sea lion swimming in the water. What can you look for to determine whether it is a seal or a sea lion?

14. What detail of cetacean birth minimizes the risk of the calf drowning?

15. A migratory marine mammal does not experience delayed implantation. What is the approximate gestation period for its young?

TEST FOR MODULE #8

1. Define the following terms:

a. Ecology   e. Limiting resource
b. Abiotic   f. Detritus
c. Biotic   g. Productivity
d. Carrying capacity   h. Carbon fixation

2. A certain species of fish feeds exclusively on green macroalgae within an ecosystem. Suppose there was a drastic change in an abiotic factor of the ecosystem that did not directly affect the fish. Could the fish population still be affected? How?

3. Give two factors that keep most populations in creation from experiencing a population explosion.

4. A species of lobster inhabits the crevices beneath a fringing coral-reef ecosystem. There are few openings under the corals, and every nook seems to be filled with a lobster. Is this struggle for living space an example of intraspecific or interspecific competition?

5. If a company is considering mass-harvesting a natural population of a specific organism, why is it important to know the organism's feeding habits as well as its predators?

6. a. The dinoflagellates called zooxanthellae are in a symbiotic relationship with coral. What type of symbiosis is this?

    b. Cleaner fishes set up stations in the ocean, where they will feed on parasites and dead tissue of other fishes. What type of symbiosis is this?

    c. What is the difference between these two examples of symbiosis?

7. Name the trophic levels in the following food chain: kelp, sea urchins, sea otters. In an ecological pyramid, which level has the most energy and largest population?

8. Is detritus a completely nonliving material?

9. Explain why knowing the primary productivity within an ecosystem does not help a scientist to guess the population of phytoplankton in that system.

10. What is the one important difference between the carbon cycle and the nitrogen cycle?

11. Describe the difference between a benthic organism and a pelagic organism.

12. Where is the aphotic zone in the ocean?

13. A benthic organism never sees sunlight, but it lives on the continental shelf. In what region of the ocean does it live?

14. In an aquarium, if there are not enough of a certain type of bacteria, the wastes from the fish cause a rise in the ammonia levels in the tank, which can harm the fish. In our discussion of the nitrogen cycle, what did we call the process by which these bacteria get rid of the ammonia?

15. In the carbon cycle, what gets rid of dissolved carbon dioxide in the ecosystem?

TEST FOR MODULE #9

1. Define the following terms:

a. Intertidal zone   d. Vertical zonation
b. Sessile   e. Ecological succession
c. Desiccated

2. What are the two major types of substrates in the intertidal zone?

3. Name one difficulty and one benefit of wave action for creatures living in the intertidal zone.

4. Name a strategy that a non-sessile intertidal organism must employ during high tide in order to avoid being thrashed about by the waves.

5. If a sessile organism cannot endure desiccation, how does it avoid desiccation in the upper intertidal area during low tide?

6. On a clear summer day, how will the temperature and salinity change in a tide pool during low tide?

7. Explain why a wave will bend, or refract, toward the shore if it approaches the shore at an angle.

8. If a beach has a canyon or sand bar offshore, will it have weak or strong wave action?

9. Why is space such an important factor to organisms in the intertidal?

10. Would salinity and temperature affect the upper or lower limits of living space for an intertidal organism?

11. In two different intertidal locations, a scientist finds bands of mussels. He notices that one location has sea stars present, while the other does not. In which location would you expect the band of mussels to be wider?

12. Once an intertidal area has reached a climax community, does this mean that no other organisms can ever move in? Why or why not?

13. Which zone of the rocky intertidal has the greatest diversity of organisms – the upper, middle, or lower intertidal?

14. What is the limiting resource of each of the three intertidal zones?

15. Which type of sediment allows water to move through more slowly – sand or mud? Why?

16. Why is zonation not noticeable in the muddy intertidal?

TEST FOR MODULE #10

1. Define the following terms:

a. Estuary
b. Euryhaline
c. Stenohaline
d. Brackish

e. Wetlands
f. Mudflats
g. Meiofauna
h. Channels

2. What caused the ocean levels of the world to rise enough to form most of the world's estuaries?

3. What is the most common substrate of an estuary? Why?

4. Why does an estuary have fluctuating salinity levels?

5. The figure below is a side-on view of a hypothetical estuary. Starting at the three X's in the figure, draw lines that delineate the salinity levels marked in the figure.

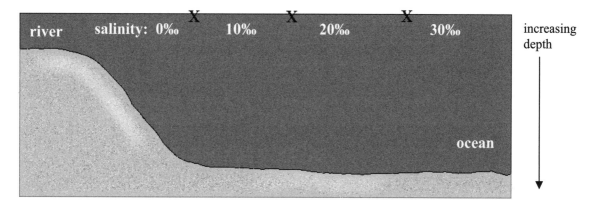

6. A scientist is studying an estuary in the Southern Hemisphere. If he is floating on a boat in the ocean and looking toward the shore, which side of the river will have the lowest salinity near the ocean?

7. A species of clam is found only in a narrow area of the center of an estuary. Is it most likely euryhaline, stenohaline, or a brackish species? Why?

8. Are salt marshes found in temperate or tropical climates?

9. What do the pneumatophores of black mangroves provide for the plants?

10. You are lost in a mangrove forest. If you are surrounded by white mangrove trees, are you at a relatively low, medium, or high elevation?

11. Why do some types of bacteria do well in the mudflats?

12. Explain why there are very few macroscopic species living on the surface of mudflats.

13. What is the relationship between the length of shorebirds' bills and the buried depths of estuarine organisms?

14. Why are channels ideal as nurseries for fishes?

15. As a rule, do estuaries provide less, just enough, or more organic material than needed for the organisms living there? If they do not provide enough, where do they get the rest, and if they provide too much, where does the excess go?

TEST FOR MODULE #11

1. Define the following terms:

a. Corallite   d. Fringing reef
b. Septa   e. Barrier reef
c. Columella   f. Atoll

2. If corals require shallow water in the warm tropics in order to grow, why are tropical areas such as the west coast of South America without reefs?

3. Explain how encrusting coralline algae aid in reef building.

4. Name a way that a coral can asexually reproduce and sexually reproduce to form another head of coral that is *not* connected to the parent coral.

5. A marine biologist is studying a coral reef that contains a large amount of branching coral. In which direction do the coral polyps mostly reproduce in order to create a branching form? In which direction do encrusting and boulder corals primarily reproduce?

6. Name one use of mucus for coral polyps.

7. Of the three regions within a fringing reef (reef flat, reef crest, and reef slope), which is the most seaward? Which is the most prolific location for coral?

8. What do scientists believe causes the "spur and groove" formations on a barrier reef?

9. What is the probable order of reef types that would form around a new oceanic volcanic island?

10. What is the name for the side of an atoll that receives the most wind and wave action?

11. Once established, a coral-reef ecosystem is nearly a self-sustaining ecosystem, requiring little outside nutrients in order to survive. Explain why.

12. What are the two major primary producers in a coral reef environment?

13. A coral reef has recently become overgrown by seaweeds. Name at least one possible reason this could have happened.

14. Name one way that a coral can attack a neighboring coral to obtain more living space.

15. The coral-reef ecosystem is a very productive as well as efficient ecosystem. How is the symbiotic relationship of mutualism a means of efficiency?

TEST FOR MODULE #12

1. Define the following terms:

a. Benthos
b. Nekton
c. Plankton

2. Would you find larger or smaller sediment particle sizes in turbulent waters? Why?

3. Where are these organisms located among the benthos: infauna, epifauna, and meiofauna?

4. What are at least two differences between the muddy-bottom soft-shelf community and the sandy-bottom soft-shelf community?

5. Detritus is the main food source in a soft-bottom shelf community. Is it vegetated or unvegetated?

6. A teacher shows you just the bottom of a green marine organism. It has roots. Is it an alga or a seagrass?

7. Since few organisms feed directly on seagrasses, how does the community take advantage of all the food they provide?

8. A shelf community has very little infauna. Do algae or seagrasses most likely grow there?

9. Name two ways that algae can defend themselves from grazers.

10. A shelf community is cold and hard-bottomed. It has a lot of sediment constantly floating in it. Would you expect to find kelp to be plentiful here?

11. Why is the third dimension of a canopy important to kelp forest organisms?

12. You see a lot of dead, floating giant kelp washing up on shore. What is the most likely explanation for this?

13. A single cell from a giant kelp has two chromosomes for each pair. Would you expect the adult from which this cell came to be large or small?

TEST FOR MODULE #13

1. Define the following terms:

a. Epipelagic zone

e. Dissolved organic matter (DOM)

b. Meroplankton

f. Microbial loop

c. Neuston

g. Upwelling

d. Vertical migration

2. Does most human activity occur in the neritic or oceanic zone of the epipelagic?

3. Distinguish between holoplankton and meroplankton.

4. Why are picoplankton important for the cycling of nutrients in the epipelagic?

5. A marine biologist does a plankton tow in the epipelagic and collects many species of zooplankton. Which organisms will most likely be the largest group collected?

6. Larvaceans are important predators in the epipelagic as well as providing an important food supply for other species. Explain their special role in the food web.

7. Most nektonic species are carnivorous predators. Give an example of a large nektonic organism that is not a carnivorous predator.

8. An epipelagic organism has many feathery projections on its body. Is it most likely planktonic or nektonic? Why?

9. Explain the benefit of swim bladders and dark, myoglobin-rich interior muscles in nektonic species such as tuna.

10. The violet shell (*Janthina*) is a predator that suspends itself upside down at the surface of the water using air-filled bubbles. Upon which group of organisms (plankton, nekton, or neuston) does this creature feed?

11. Why are most epipelagic nekton silver and blue in color?

12. Which epipelagic creatures undergo vertical migration?

13. The microbial loop is sometimes referred to as a food web within a food web. Explain why this might be so.

14. The equator has a relatively high amount of primary productivity, yet just north and south of it, productivity greatly is diminished. Explain why it is so high at the equator.

15. How is the weather in India connected to the weather in Peru and Chile?

TEST FOR MODULE #14

1. Define the following terms:

a. Mesopelagic zone   d. Bioluminescence
b. Photophores   e. Chemosynthesis
c. Hydrothermal vent

2. As depth increases in the ocean, the abundance of life and the quantity of food decrease. Explain why this is so.

3. Suppose you drop a thermometer into the ocean and monitor its temperature reading as it sinks. You suddenly notice a sharp drop in the temperature. In which zone of the ocean is the thermometer?

4. Suppose the thermometer in the question above has a pressure-sensitive device as well. Suppose you continue to watch both the pressure and the temperature as the devices continue to sink. Assuming you already saw the sharp drop in temperature mentioned in the previous problem, which would you expect to change more drastically after that point: pressure or temperature?

5. How do mesopelagic fishes compare in size to their epipelagic counterparts?

6. Why do most mesopelagic fishes have a broad diet?

7. What physical features are typically possessed by mesopelagic fish that find their food through vertical migration?

8. How are ventrally located photophores helpful in camouflage?

9. What physical feature differentiates the deep sea from the mesopelagic?

10. What two chemicals must an organism produce in order to perform bioluminescence? What does each chemical do?

11. As compared to an organism's ability to get food in the deep sea water column, how difficult is it for a deep sea floor individual to find food?

12. The figure below shows a food web for the deep sea floor. Fill in the blanks labeled a-c.

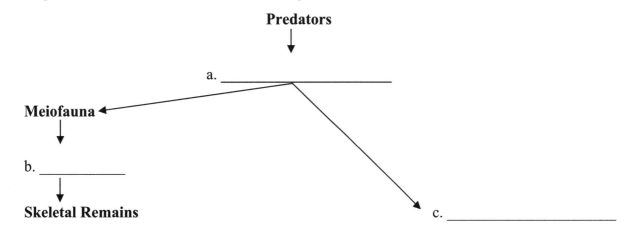

13. A marine biologist studied a sunken whale carcass at a specific location on the deep sea floor along with the organisms living on it. Just two years later, scientists returned to the same location to discover bare ocean floor. What happened to this community?

TEST FOR MODULE #15

1. Define the following terms:

a. Clupeoid fishes

c. Sustainable yield

b. Gadoid fishes

d. Mariculture

2. What is the fisheries' term used for fish that are harvested for food?

3. How does coastal upwelling enhance fish populations?

4. Which group of fishes are most often caught by purse seines?

5. Which group of fishes are most often caught by trawls?

6. In the 1950s, the Peruvian anchoveta, a clupeoid fish like the anchovy, was heavily fished for use as fish meal and oil. Anchovetas were heavily fished until the early 1970s when stocks were suddenly severely decreased, and the anchoveta fishing industry collapsed. What was the most likely cause of the decrease in anchoveta stocks?

7. Name two ways fisheries can aid overfished populations in recovering without completely halting fishing altogether.

8. Which type of mariculture involves controlling the water quality?

9. Explain why it would be difficult to raise tunas in a mariculture facility.

10. What does the term "renewable resource" mean? Give an example of a renewable marine resource.

11. What are the benefits that reverse osmosis has over distillation in desalinization?

12. In a few areas of the world, such as in Norway, there are curious-looking structures similar to windmills that are located under water. For what are they used?

TEST FOR MODULE #16

1. Define the following terms:

a. Eutrophication   c. Biomagnification
b. Nonbiodegradable   d. Fouling organisms

2. Differentiate the following activities as indirectly or directly affecting an estuary:

a. Dredging the bottom to allow larger ships access
b. Fertilizer runoff from a farm 25 miles inland
c. Filling in parts of the estuary with sand to support oceanfront property
d. Trawling for shrimp
e. Diverting river water upstream to supply fresh water for crops

3. A tropical fish dealer receives a shipment of marine fish, 90% of which die after the first week. It turns out that the collectors used cyanide to capture the fish. Besides this direct effect on the fish, what would be an indirect effect to the coral reef of the use of poison in the water?

4. Why is chlorine not the best solution for treating sewage to be dumped into the ocean?

5. Explain the following statement: Marshes are secondary purifying plants for raw sewage.

6. An ecosystem is exposed to a large oil spill, but it recovers from the exposure fairly quickly. What can you say about the wave action in this ecosystem?

7. Suppose you are looking at two difference ecosystems: an estuary and a deep-ocean seafloor. You find oil in both. Most likely, which ecosystem's oil is the result of natural processes?

8. You are looking at how two pollutants affect a marine ecosystem. Both are fat-soluble chemicals, but one is biodegradable and one is not. As you compare planktivorous fish to marine mammals in the ecosystem, which chemical will you expect to find larger quantities of in the marine mammals?

9. Chlorinated hydrocarbons are subject to biomagnification. Name another type of chemical also subject to biomagnification.

10. What type of pollutant can kill or harm *any* marine organism without being eaten?

11. How can Styrofoam® be dangerous for marine life?

12. A demolition company suggests cleaning the rubble from several buildings it has destroyed and dumping it in a shallow, sandy-bottomed area of the ocean. Although some are against this proposal, the local marine biologists are quite supportive of it. Why?

SOLUTIONS TO THE TEST FOR MODULE #1

1. (7 pts – one for each definition)

a. <u>Oceanic crust</u> – The outermost layer of the earth which contains primarily basalt, is relatively dense, and is about 5 kilometers thick

b. <u>Continental crust</u> – The outermost layer of the earth which contains primarily granite, is less dense than oceanic crust, and is 20-50 kilometers thick

c. <u>Mid-ocean ridge</u> – A continuous chain of underwater volcanic mountains encompassing the earth

d. <u>Subduction</u> – The downward movement of one plate into the earth's mantle when two plates collide

e. <u>Salinity</u> – The total amount of salt dissolved in a solvent

f. <u>Coriolis effect</u> – The way in which the rotation of the earth bends the path of winds and resulting sea currents

g. <u>Gyres</u> – Large, mostly circular systems of surface currents driven by the wind

2. (1 pt) <u>The organism could move from one ocean basin to another because they are interconnected by the Southern Ocean, which continually surrounds Antarctica.</u>

3. (1 pt) Oceanic crust is under water <u>because it is denser than continental crust and "floats" lower on the semi-plastic mantle.</u>

4. (2 pts – one for mentioning that plates move apart, one for mentioning the mantle material rising up) <u>As two plates of the earth's crust move away from one another, there is less pressure on the mantle below the resulting rift. This allows the mantle material to rise up, cool, and become new oceanic crust.</u>

5. (1 pt) <u>More sunlight can penetrate to the seafloor in the shallower depths and therefore more plant life can survive.</u> This provides an opportunity for more animal life to survive also.

6. (1 pt – The student only needs to list one of the following.) <u>Hydrogen bonding keeps the boiling point and the freezing point of water from being excessively low. It makes ice less dense than liquid water, causing it to float on the surface and keeping the organisms below the ice alive. It causes water to have a high specific heat, preventing extreme fluctuations in the water temperature. Lastly, it can dissolve a large number of solvents, including salts.</u>

7. (2 pts – one for the effect of salinity and one for the effect of temperature) <u>Higher salinity increases water's density, and lower temperatures increase water's density.</u>

8. (2 pts – one for less life and one for why) <u>Less. The greater material suspended in the water makes the water less transparent and prevents the penetration of light. This would prohibit many producers from growing and therefore result in the presence of fewer animals.</u>

9. (1 pt) The currents of the ocean are driven by <u>the wind</u>. Since heat from the sun causes the winds, you could also say the sun.

10. (1 pt) <u>The gyre in the northern Atlantic Ocean</u> brings warmer, equatorial water to North Carolina and colder, arctic water to Portugal.

11. (2 pts – one for the tidal range and one for the reason) <u>A spring tide is a time of largest tidal range due to the combined effects of the gravitational pulls of the aligned sun and moon, while a neap tide is a time of smallest tidal range due to the gravitational pulls of the moon and the sun working 90 degrees from one another.</u>

12. (1 pt) The <u>thermocline</u> separates the surface layer from the deep layer of the ocean, so the organism would have to cross it.

Total possible points: 22

SOLUTIONS TO THE TEST FOR MODULE #2

1. (7 pts – one for each definition)

a. <u>Autotrophs</u> – Organisms that are able to produce their own food

b. <u>Heterotrophs</u> – Organisms that cannot make their own food and must obtain it from other organisms

c. <u>Respiration</u> – The process by which food is converted in to useable energy for life functions

d. <u>Homeostasis</u> – The tendency of living organisms to control or regulate changes in their internal environment

e. <u>Poikilotherm</u> – An organism whose body temperature changes with its surrounding environment

f. <u>Homeotherm</u> – An animal that maintains a controlled internal body temperature using its own heating and cooling mechanisms

g. <u>Binomial nomenclature</u> – Identifying an organism by its genus and species name

2. (4 pts – one for each group) The four main groups of molecules involved in metabolism are <u>carbohydrates, proteins, lipids, and nucleic acids.</u>

3. (2 pts – one for the effect on oxygen and one for the effect on carbon dioxide) Algae are responsible for most of the photosynthesis in Creation. Since photosynthesis uses carbon dioxide and produces oxygen, <u>the amount of oxygen in the atmosphere would probably increase, while the amount of carbon dioxide in the atmosphere would decrease.</u>

4. (1 pt) They would be <u>autotrophs</u> since they can produce their own food.

5. (1 pt) <u>You cannot.</u> Both prokaryotes and eukaryotes can have structures that move them through the water (flagella), so this information would not be enough to distininguish this organism.

6. (1 pt) <u>An organ is made up of several tissues performing as a functional unit</u>.

7. (1 pt) The <u>plasma membrane</u> is selectively permeable, hindering specific molecules from passing through it.

8. (1 pt) <u>No</u>. An osmoregulator deals with changes in its environment so as to keeps the composition of its body fluids constant. The body fluids of an osmoconformer would change.

9. (1 pt) A large tuna can maintain a warmer body temperature by <u>retaining the heat produced by its large muscles, enabling it to stay active even in cold water.</u>

10. (1 pt) They are most likely a result of <u>asexual reproduction</u> because by broadcasting gametes into the water, the fertilized eggs would then float to a different location before they settle.

11. (1 pt) <u>The two organisms were not of the same species</u>, despite the fact that they appeared similar. In order to be of the same species, two organisms must be able to reproduce fertile offspring.

Total possible points: 21

SOLUTIONS TO THE TEST FOR MODULE #3

1. (8 pts – one for each definition)

a. <u>Bacteria</u> – Prokaryotic, single-celled, microscopic organisms

b. <u>Decomposers</u> – Organisms that break down dead organic matter into smaller molecules

c. <u>Phytoplankton</u> – Microscopic photosynthetic organisms that drift in the water

d. <u>Zooplankton</u> – Tiny floating organisms that are either small animals or protozoa

e. <u>Thallus</u> – The complete body of an alga, not differentiated into true leaves, stems, or roots

f. <u>Haploid</u> – A cell that contains half the normal number of chromosomes

g. <u>Diploid</u> – A cell that contains two similar sets of chromosomes

h. <u>Symbiosis</u> – A close relationship between two species where at least one benefits

2. (2 pts – one for each process) <u>Photosynthesis and chemosynthesis</u> are two processes that autotrophic bacteria use to convert energy into organic matter.

3. (1 pt) <u>These plant-like organisms are prokaryotic and therefore more like bacteria.</u>

4. (2 pts – one for each benefit) <u>Diatoms produce large amounts of the world's oxygen and their fossilized shells can be mined for many commercial products.</u> The student could just name two commercial products as well, such as toothpaste and filters.

5. (1 pt) <u>It is most likely a deposit of fossilized diatomaceous ooze (diatomaceous earth). These deposits are formed as ocean sediments.</u>

6. (1 pt) <u>Some blooms are due to planktonic organisms that produce toxic substances that can poison fish that people eat.</u>

7. (1 pt) <u>Pneumatocysts help the blades of the thallus float on water.</u> This maximizes their exposure to sunlight so as to maximize their photosynthesis.

8. (2 pts – one for the algae and one for the function) <u>Brown algae</u> contain algin, which <u>helps substances stay mixed together.</u>

9. (2 pts – one for gametophyte and one for haploid) In alternation of generations, the generations alternate between sporophyte and gametophyte. The sporophyte generation releases spores. Thus, spores always develop into the <u>gametophyte</u> generation. That generation will be <u>haploid,</u> as spores produce organisms with the same number of chromosomes as the spores themselves. Only gametes produce organisms with a different number of chromosomes, because two gametes must fuse to become a new organism. As a result, gametes always produce diploid organisms after fertilization.

10. (1 pt – ½ for each organism) A lichen is made up of <u>a fungus and an alga.</u>

11. (1 pt) <u>Seagrasses do not need to attract pollinators to spread their pollen. They release it in the ocean currents.</u>

12. (1 pt) The red mangrove's <u>prop roots</u> help accumulate sediments.

Total possible points: 23

SOLUTIONS TO THE TEST FOR MODULE #4

1. (8 pts – one for each definition)

a. <u>Amoebocytes</u> – Cells within a sponge that produce its skeletal structure, perform digestion, and repair cell damage

b. <u>Metamorphosis</u> – A complete morphological change from larval to adult form

c. <u>Polyp</u> – An attached cnidarian stage, appearing sac-like or barrel-like

d. <u>Medusa</u> – A free-swimming cnidarian stage, appearing bell-like or umbrella-like

e. <u>Mesoglea</u> – A jelly-like substance between the inner layer and outer layer of cells in a cnidarian

f. <u>Mutualism</u> – A relationship between two or more organisms of different species where both benefit from the association

g. <u>Commensalism</u> – A relationship between two or more organisms of different species where one benefits and the other is neither harmed nor benefited

h. <u>Parasitism</u> – A relationship between two or more organisms of different species where one benefits and the other is harmed

2. (2 pts – one for a radially symmetric organism and one for a bilaterally symmetric organism)
   Radial symmetry – <u>Hydrozoans, corals, jellyfish, anemones, or comb jellies</u>
   Bilateral symmetry – <u>flatworms, turbellarians, flukes, tapeworms, or any other worm in this module</u>

3. (2 pts – one for each answer) Sponges can have elastic protein fibers called <u>spongin</u> and calcium carbonate or silica <u>spicules</u> for support.

4. (1 pt) <u>They produce planktonic larvae that float to new areas of the ocean.</u>

5. (3 pts – one for each characteristic. Take one point off for any characteristics not on this list) <u>They both have (1) an oral side, (2) an aboral side, (3) a central mouth, (4) a mouth surrounded by tentacles, (5) stinging nematocysts, and (6) a gut with a single opening.</u> The student only needs to mention three.

6. (1 pt) The <u>scyphozoa, or jellyfish,</u> spend most of their lives as medusae.

7. (1 pt) <u>Only the outside surface of a coral reef is actually alive.</u> The inside is made up of skeletons of previous generations of coral polyps.

8. (1 pt) <u>It is most likely bilaterally symmetric,</u> as bilaterally symmetric organisms have more complex nervous systems.

9. (1 pt) <u>It is a tapeworm.</u> Since tapeworms are parasites living in the intestines of their hosts, their hosts digest the food, and the tapeworms just absorb the nutrients into their bodies.

10. (1 pt) There are a few examples of parasites in this module: <u>flukes, tapeworms, roundworms, and leeches</u>. The student needs only list one.

11. (1 pt) This animal would be in phylum <u>Annelida</u>.

12. (1 pt) A lophophore is a <u>crown of ciliated tentacles used for feeding</u>.

Total possible points: 23

SOLUTIONS TO THE TEST FOR MODULE #5

1. (8 pts – one for each definition)

a. <u>Mantle</u> – A sheath of tissue surrounding the organs of a mollusk, producing the mollusk's shell and performing respiration

b. <u>Radula</u> – An organ covered with hundreds of small teeth used for scraping food into the mouths of mollusks

c. <u>Chitin</u> – A derivative of carbohydrates that provides both flexibility and support

d. <u>Molting</u> – The process of shedding an exoskeleton and replacing it with a new one

e. <u>Cephalothorax</u> – The anterior part of an arthropod body, consisting of a head and other body segments fused together

f. <u>Carapace</u> – An armored shield that covers the anterior portion of crustaceans

g. <u>Ambulacral groove</u> – A channel along the oral surface of echinoderms through which the tube feet protrude

h. <u>Dorsal nerve cord</u> – A long bundle of nerve cells located along the dorsal part of an organism's body

2. (2 pts – one for each characteristic) Most mollusks have a <u>mantle</u> for shell production and respiration, and a <u>radula</u> for feeding. The student could also say <u>a shell, gills, and a foot</u>.

3. (3 pts – the student needs one example for each class) Some examples of a gastropod are a <u>snail, an abalone, and a limpet</u>. Some examples of a bivalve are a <u>clam, an oyster, and a scallop</u>. Some examples of a cephalopod are an <u>octopus, a squid, and a cuttlefish</u>.

4. (8 pts – one for each structure) a. <u>muscle</u> b. <u>mouth</u> c. <u>foot</u> d. <u>gut</u> e. <u>heart</u> f. <u>siphons</u> g. <u>gills</u> h. <u>mantle</u>

5. (1 pt) The shrimp <u>must have recently molted</u>. You found the shed exoskeleton in the aquarium. The live shrimp must be hiding among the rocks until its new, larger exoskeleton hardens.

6. (1 pt) <u>Cleaner shrimp set up stations where they pick off and eat parasites and organic material from the fish. The fish benefit by the removal of the detrimental parasites, and the shrimp benefit by obtaining an easy meal</u>.

7. (1 pt) <u>When the females do meet a male, the male will transfer sperm directly to the female, who will store it to fertilize many batches of eggs</u>. Therefore they do not need to come into contact with a male each time they produce a batch of eggs.

8. (1 pt) <u>It is a network of water-filled canals that operates the organism's tube feet</u>. The tube feet provide locomotion and feeding functions, as well as sensory, respiratory and excretory duties.

9. (1 pt) <u>The sea cucumber was put under stress, so it instinctively eviscerated a portion of its insides.</u> This is to provide would-be predators with an easy snack, giving time for the sea cucumber to hide. <u>This process does not hurt the animal because it can regenerate the lost tissue.</u>

10. (2 pts – one for the sea urchins and one for the sea cucumbers) <u>The sea urchins feed on tough-to-digest algae and marine grasses. They therefore need a longer digestive tract to process them. Sea cucumbers swallow sediments as they crawl along the ocean floor. Their long gut allows for sorting the food out of the sediments.</u>

11. (1 pt) <u>Echinoderm gametes are usually released during a short season of the year.</u> This increases their chances of finding another gamete with which they can fuse for fertilization.

12. (1 pt) <u>It is a flexible rod that provides support for an animal. The adult tunicates have a leather-like tunic for support.</u>

13. (2 pts – one for each answer) The student need name only two: <u>sea squirts, ascidians, salps, and lancelets</u>.

14. (4 pts – one for each part)

a. A radula is in organisms from the phylum <u>Mollusca. Its purpose is for scraping food into their mouths</u>.

b. An exoskeleton is in organisms from the phylum <u>Arthropoda. It provides support to the body</u>.

c. A water vascular system is in organisms from the phylum <u>Echinodermata. It mobilizes tube feet for locomotion and feeding</u>.

d. A notochord is in organisms from the phylum <u>Chordata. It provides support for the body</u>.

Total possible points: 36

SOLUTIONS TO THE TEST FOR MODULE #6

1. (5 pts – one for each definition)

a. <u>Demersal</u> – Fishes that live on the bottom of the ocean.

b. <u>Chromatophores</u> – Surface pigment cells that expand and contract to produce various colors

c. <u>Hermaphroditism</u> – A situation in which an animal has the reproductive organs of both sexes

d. <u>Oviparous</u> – A type of development in which eggs are hatched outside a female's body

e. <u>Viviparous</u> – A type of development in which the young obtain their nutrients directly from the mother and are birthed live

2. (2 pts – one for each characteristic) Agnathans do not have <u>jaws, scales, paired fins, or true bones</u>. The student need list only two of these.

3. (1 pt) <u>Lampreys are anadromous</u>. They are hatched in fresh water rivers and streams, then move into the ocean as adults. They then return to fresh water in order to reproduce. <u>Some scientists consider lampreys to be primitive fish, yet they display this advanced migration behavior.</u>

4. (1 pt) It must be a <u>ray</u>. If it has a jaw, it cannot be a lamprey, as lampreys are jawless fish. It cannot be a bony fish, however, since it has no osteocytes or osteoblasts, which are necessary for a skeleton to be made of bones.

5. (1 pt – one for each characteristic) They are <u>flat</u> so that they can move across the ocean bottom. Their <u>mouths are located ventrally</u> for convenient feeding, and their <u>eyes are on the dorsal side of their bodies</u>. The student need mention only two of these.

6. (1 pt) An <u>operculum</u> closes while water is let into the gills via the bony fish's mouth. This keeps water from flowing back in over the gills from the rear. This ensures the countercurrent system of the gills.

7. (1 pt) It has a <u>swim bladder</u> in which the amount of gas can be regulated.

8. (3 pts – one for each characteristic) A bony fish has an <u>operculum instead of gill slits, comparatively large scales, fins with rays, and a terminal mouth</u>. <u>Bony fish also have bone, while cartilaginous fish have only cartilage</u>. The student need mention only three.

9. (1 pt) This is an example of <u>disguise</u>. The spot confuses predator fish, making them think that the tail end of the fish is the head end.

10. (1 pt) The spiral intestine is <u>a portion of the shark's intestine that provides a great deal of surface area with its spiraling interior, and yet it takes up very little space</u>.

11. (1 pt) Fishes have a <u>countercurrent system</u> of blood flow.

12. (2 pts – one for movement and one for electrical current) They are <u>sensory organs that help sharks detect movement in the water as well as tiny electrical currents emitted by a fish's movement</u>.

13. (1 pt) <u>Anadromous behavior is when fishes migrate from saltwater to reproduce in fresh water. Catadromous behavior is when fishes migrate from fresh water to reproduce in saltwater.</u>

14. (1 pt) This fish is probably <u>ovoviviparous</u>, since an oviparous fish lays lots of eggs so that at least a few hatch.

15. (8 pts – one for each structure) a. <u>nare</u> b. <u>spiracle</u> c. <u>lateral line</u> d. <u>dorsal fins</u> e. <u>anal fin</u> f. <u>pelvic fins</u> g. <u>pectoral fins</u> h. <u>gill slits</u>

Total possible points: 30

SOLUTIONS TO THE TEST FOR MODULE #7

1. (5 pts – one for each definition)

a. <u>Adaptation</u> – An expression of a helpful trait coming directly from the genetic information already possessed by at least some individuals in a genetically diverse population

b. <u>Baleen</u> – Rows of comb-like horny plates that project from the upper jaws of filter-feeding whales

c. <u>Echolocation</u> – A method of analyzing sound waves to locate objects in the water column

d. <u>Behavior</u> – An activity an organism would do in its natural habitat

e. <u>Delayed implantation</u> – A delay in implantation of an embryo into the uterus, allowing for the proper timing of birth

2. (1 pt) <u>Sea-turtle hatchlings must make a journey from where they hatch on the shore to the water. During that time, they are easy pickings for birds, so predatory birds tend to come to shore for an easy meal.</u>

3. (1 pt) It helps <u>remove excess salts from the body</u>.

4. (1 pt) <u>A flat tail aids in swimming.</u> Sea snakes spend their lives swimming, while marine iguanas must swim for their food.

5. (1 pt) <u>You tend to find marine reptiles in warmer climates</u>, because they are ectothermic.

6. (1 pt) <u>The extra webbing of their feet helps them in swimming.</u>

7. (1 pt) The only other type of whale is a toothed whale. <u>If the jaw has no teeth, it is from a baleen whale</u>.

8. (1 pt) To support such a large body, they must be feeding at an almost continuous rate. <u>The large quantity of readily available plankton in the ocean is an excellent food source. Filter-feeders also avoid expending a great deal of energy having to hunt prey.</u> They student need list only one reason.

9. (1 pt) The manatees and dugongs in <u>order Sirenia spend their entire lives in the water</u>. The animals in orders Pinnipedia (seals and sea lions) and Carnivora (sea otters and polar bears) spend at least some of their time on land.

10. (1 pt) You would find it on a <u>toothed whale</u>. The melon is a part of the echolocation system of a whale, and only toothed whales use echolocation. A baleen whale does not need echolocation, as it does not need to "hunt" for plankton. They are everywhere.

11. (3 pts – one for what makes the clicks, one for what the melon does, and one for what happens to the sounds coming back) <u>At their blowholes are muscular valves called nasal plugs that control air pressure while the dolphin is making clicks, which come from the muscles of the dolphin's air sacs. The clicks are aimed forward toward the front of the skull and focused out of the head by the dolphin's</u>

melon. Sounds coming back are received by the lower jaw, which transmits the vibrations to sensitive inner ears. The information finally goes to the brain, where it is turned into a "picture."

12. (1 pt) A dolphin's flexible rib cage collapses under great pressure, pushing air that is in the lungs to other parts of its body. This prevents the air from dissolving into the blood stream.

13. (1 pt) Look for external ears. Seals just have holes that allow sound into their inner ears. Sea lions have external structures around those holes.

14. (1 pt) The calf is born tail first. It is also led to the surface by the mother or another individual.

15. (1 pt) The gestation period is most likely a year. Since the mammal reaches the breeding ground only once per year, it must either have delayed implantation or a gestation period of a year in order for the calf to be born at the breeding grounds.

Total possible points: 21

SOLUTIONS TO THE TEST FOR MODULE #8

1. (8 pts – one for each definition)

a. <u>Ecology</u> – The study of the relationship between an organism and its environment

b. <u>Abiotic</u> – The nonliving part of an environment

c. <u>Biotic</u> – The living part of an environment

d. <u>Carrying capacity</u> – The largest population size that can be supported by a specific area with its available resources

e. <u>Limiting resource</u> – A factor required for a population to grow, but present in small quantities in an ecosystem

f. <u>Detritus</u> – Dead organic matter and the decomposing organisms living among it

g. <u>Productivity</u> – The rate of photosynthesis in an ecosystem

h. <u>Carbon fixation</u> – Converting inorganic carbon into useful organic carbon

2. (2 pts – one for yes, one for why) <u>Yes. The abiotic factor, such as salinity or temperature, could affect the macroalgae population, possibly reducing its numbers, and thus indirectly affect the fish populations by reducing the amount of available food.</u>

3. (2 pts – the student needs to either mention at least two factors or use the terms "biotic" and "abiotic") Populations will usually not explode because <u>abiotic factors</u> (such as storms, water temperature, and salinity) and <u>biotic factors</u> (such as insufficient nutrients or presence of predators) <u>control their size</u>.

4. (1 pt) Since the lobsters are members of the same species, this is an example of <u>intraspecific competition</u>.

5. (1 pt) It is important because <u>their populations are all dependent upon one another</u>. When a population is greatly decreased, the population of the organisms it feeds upon may begin to rapidly *increase*. And the population of predators that feed upon the harvested organism may begin to *decrease* due to lack of available food.

6. (3 pts – one for each part)

a. <u>Mutualism</u>

b. This is also <u>mutualism</u>.

c. The difference between these two associations is that <u>in the second relationship, although both organisms benefit from their association, they do not need each other to survive. In the first example, the zooxanthellae and the coral need each other to survive.</u>

7. (2 pts – one for the three trophic levels and one for the primary producers having the most energy) The kelp is the primary producer. The sea urchins are the primary consumers. The sea otters are the secondary consumers. The primary producers have the most energy and, most likely, the largest population.

8. (1 pt) No, detritus is composed of dead organic matter along with the decomposing organisms that live among it. So it is not *completely* made of nonliving material.

9. (1 pt) Some phytoplankton are more productive than others. One area of an ecosystem, then, could have a high primary productivity due to a low number of very productive phytoplankton.

10. (1 pt) In the nitrogen cycle, naturally occurring nitrogen gas is not in a usable form for most organisms. Therefore, it must be fixed by bacteria or blue-green algae before it can enter the cycle. In the carbon cycle, many organisms can directly utilize naturally occurring carbon dioxide gas to fix the carbon.

11. (1 pt) A benthic organism lives at the ocean bottom, while a pelagic organism lives up in the water column.

12. (1 pt) It is the area of ocean where light cannot penetrate and therefore no photosynthesis can occur.

13. (1 pt) It lives on the outer shelf. That's the only part of the continental shelf that does not get sunlight.

14. (1 pt) We called it denitrification. This converts nitrogen in the form of ammonia back to gaseous nitrogen, which the nitrogen-fixing bacteria can then work on.

15. (1 pt) Photosynthesis by the producers gets rid of the dissolved carbon dioxide.

Total possible points: 27

SOLUTIONS TO THE TEST FOR MODULE #9

1. (5 pts – one for each answer)

a. <u>Intertidal zone</u> – The area of shoreline between high and low tides

b. <u>Sessile</u> – A member of the epifauna that lives attached to a substrate

c. <u>Desiccated</u> – A term referring to an organism that has lost its body moisture

d. <u>Vertical zonation</u> – Noticeable horizontal bands of organisms living within a certain range in the intertidal zone

e. <u>Ecological succession</u> – A gradual, increasing occupation of new organisms into a specific area

2. (2 pts – one for each answer) The two intertidal substrates are <u>rocky and sandy/muddy</u>.

3. (2 pts – one for a problem, one for a benefit) Wave action can <u>wash away any organisms that cannot hold onto the substrate</u>. It can also <u>push rocks and debris into organisms, crushing them</u>. But waves can <u>wash away accumulated wastes and bring nutrients into an area</u>. The student need list only one of each.

4. (1 pt) <u>It either must move to a crevice where it is protected from the wave action, or it must firmly cling to a hard substrate</u>. The student need list only one.

5. (1 pt) <u>It must be able to seal moisture within its body or in a crack in the substrate</u>. The main point is sealing in moisture.

6. (1 pt – ½ for each effect) <u>The temperature will most likely rise from the summer heat, and the salinity will rise due to water evaporation</u>.

7. (1 pt) <u>The part of the wave closest to the shore will slow down when it enters shallow water. The other end of the wave will still be traveling at the original speed, and will therefore cause the wave to bend toward the shore until it is nearly parallel to it</u>.

8. (1 pt) Canyons divert waves away from the shore, and sandbars protect the shore from waves. Thus, the shore will have <u>weak wave action</u>.

9. (1 pt) To survive in the intertidal, <u>organisms must have a location on which to hang, or they get washed away</u>.

10. (1 pt) These are abiotic factors, which affect the <u>upper limits</u>.

11. (1 pt) The location <u>without the sea stars would have a wider band of mussels because there are no sea stars to prey on them</u>.

12. (2 pts – one for the no, one for the explanation) <u>No</u>, new space can be created in a climax community by various <u>biotic factors</u> (predation, competition) <u>and abiotic factors</u> (extreme temperature or salinity changes), <u>that kill off existing organisms</u>.

13. (1 pt) The <u>lower intertidal</u> has the most diversity because it is under water the longest of the three areas and therefore more organisms can survive there.

14. (3 pts – one for each) The limiting resource of the upper intertidal is <u>water</u>; the middle intertidal is <u>space</u>; and the lower intertidal are <u>space and light</u>.

15. (2 pts – one for mud, one for the explanation) <u>Mud</u> allows water to move through more slowly <u>because the smaller particles are closer together</u>.

16. (1 pt) Zonation is not noticeable because <u>most of the organisms living there are buried</u> (infauna) to keep from being washed away by the waves.

Total possible points: 26

SOLUTIONS TO THE TEST FOR MODULE #10

1. (8 pts – one for each answer)

a. <u>Estuary</u> – A semi-enclosed area at the mouth of a river where fresh water and seawater meet and mix

b. <u>Euryhaline</u> – Species that can tolerate a wide range of salinities

c. <u>Stenohaline</u> – Species that can tolerate a narrow range of salinities

d. <u>Brackish</u> – Water that is less salty than seawater but saltier than fresh water

e. <u>Wetlands</u> – Estuarine areas of high elevations that are periodically covered with water

f. <u>Mudflats</u> – Wide expanses of an estuary that are exposed during low tide

g. <u>Meiofauna</u> – Microscopic organisms living in between marine sediment particles

h. <u>Channels</u> – Estuarine areas where water is present both during high and low tides

2. (1 pt) The world's ocean levels rose from <u>the melting of large quantities of ice from an ice age</u>.

3. (1 pt) The most common substrate of an estuary is <u>mud because of the constant deposition of silt and clay eroded from upriver and put down in the estuary</u>.

4. (1 pt) Because there is <u>constant mixing of fresh water flowing out to the ocean and salty ocean water moving in with the tide</u>. The student can also include evaporation in shallow estuaries.

5. (1 pt – $\frac{1}{3}$ for each line) The main thing to realize is that estuaries have salt wedges. The student's lines do not have to be exactly like those below, but they must be diagonal so that the lower depths have higher salinities.

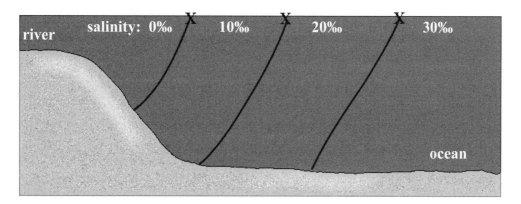

6. (1 pt) The rule says that the lowest salinity parts of the river will be on the <u>left</u> in the Southern Hemisphere.

7. (2 pts – one for brackish, one for the explanation) It is most likely a <u>brackish species</u>. Euryhaline species would live throughout an estuary, tolerating wide ranges of salinities, and stenohaline species would be found either near the ocean or river side of the estuary, tolerating only narrow ranges of salinities. <u>Brackish species can tolerate about half the salinity of seawater, which is probably found in the center of the estuary.</u>

8. (1 pt) They are found in <u>temperate climates</u>.

9. (1 pt) They allow for <u>more exposure to oxygen</u>.

10. (1 pt) You are at a relatively <u>high elevation</u>, because white mangrove trees are not very tolerant of salt and thus must stay at higher elevations.

11. (1 pt) <u>They can survive the anaerobic conditions of the muddy substrate, feeding on the plentiful organic matter.</u>

12. (1 pt) <u>There is little, if any, hard substrate on which to attach. Plus, there would be exposure to air and predators.</u> Either answer is fine.

13. (1 pt) The bill length of a shore bird determines the organism it can reach as it probes the mud for food. <u>Longer bills can reach deeply buried organisms, while shorter bills can reach shallower organisms.</u>

14. (1 pt) <u>Channels provide large quantities of food for juvenile fishes, in the form of plankton. They also are protected geographically from predators.</u> The student need list only one.

15. (2 pts – one for more, one for where it goes) Estuaries provide <u>more</u> organic material than needed for the organisms living there. <u>The excess flows out into nearby ecosystems</u> via a process called outwelling.

Total possible points: 24

SOLUTIONS TO THE TEST FOR MODULE #11

1. (6 pts – one for each answer)

a. <u>Corallite</u> – The cup-shaped calcium skeleton in which a coral polyp sits

b. <u>Septa</u> – A series of sharp ridges radiating from the center of a corallite cup

c. <u>Columella</u> – Central projections from the floor of a corallite cup

d. <u>Fringing reef</u> – A type of coral reef that forms as a border along the coast

e. <u>Barrier reef</u> – A type of coral reef that occurs at a distance from the coast

f. <u>Atoll</u> – A ring of coral reef with steep outer slopes and enclosing a shallow lagoon

2. (1 pt) <u>The Coriolis effect causes cold polar currents to move into the tropics on the western coast of</u> <u>South America</u> (as well as some other tropical continental coasts). Corals cannot survive in the cooler water.

3. (1 pt) <u>Coralline algae create a hard sediment out of soft sediments by growing over and trapping</u> <u>fine, soft sediments, which include shells and rubble from reef organisms.</u>

4. (2 pts – one for each answer) When a piece of <u>coral is broken off</u> (as a result of a storm, for example) the living polyps on that piece can continue to reproduce and grow, forming a new coral head not connected to the original coral head. Also, when corals sexually reproduce, the <u>spawned larvae</u> eventually settle out of the water column and metamorphose into a polyp that can reproduce into a new, separate coral head.

5. (2 pts – one for each answer) The branching coral primarily reproduces in an <u>upward direction</u>; the polyps pull themselves up out of the corallite and secrete a new elevated bottom. Encrusting and boulder corals mainly reproduce in a <u>sideways direction</u> by polyps pinching off portions of their bodies and creating a new, neighboring polyp.

6. (1 pt) Secreted mucus is used for <u>transferring food to the polyp's mouth</u> via the motion of cilia. Also, mucus is used to <u>trap sediments</u> and move them off the polyp again via the motion of cilia. The student need name only one.

7. (2 pts – one for each answer) The <u>reef slope</u> is the most seaward region on a fringing reef. The most prolific area is the <u>reef crest</u>.

8. (1 pt) Spur-and-groove formations are most likely caused by <u>strong wind and wave movement</u>.

9. (1 pt) The order would be <u>fringing reef, barrier reef, and atoll</u>.

10. (1 pt) It is called the <u>windward</u> side.

11. (1 pt) <u>The coral reef efficiently recycles its nutrients and produces its own fixed nitrogen.</u>

12. (2 pts – one for each answer) The two major primary producers are <u>zooxanthellae and seaweeds</u>.

13. (1 pt) <u>Excess nutrients could be in the water</u> (as a result of waste or fertilizer runoff from land), which would feed the seaweeds. Or there could be a <u>reduction in the population of fish that graze on the seaweeds</u>. The student need list only one.

14. (1 pt) It can use <u>digestive filaments to eat the tissue of the neighboring coral or it can use stinging tentacles to injure its neighbor</u>. It can also <u>grow over its neighbor, blocking out the light</u>. The student need list only one.

15. (1 pt) The <u>cohabitation of species enables twice as many organisms to live in the same area</u>. Therefore, it is a more efficient use of limited space.

Total possible points: 24

SOLUTIONS TO THE TEST FOR MODULE #12

1. (3 pts – one for each answer)

a. <u>Benthos</u> – Marine organisms that live on the sea bottom

b. <u>Nekton</u> – Marine organisms that swim strongly enough to move against the ocean current

c. <u>Plankton</u> – Marine organisms that cannot swim strongly enough to move against the ocean current

2. (1 pt) You would find <u>larger sediment particles in areas with strong wave action because the currents would move the finer particles away.</u>

3. (3 pts – one for each location) <u>Infauna are buried in the sediment, epifauna are on the surface of the sediment, and meiofauna are in between the sediment particles.</u>

4. (2 pts – one for each contrasting pair) <u>The muddy-bottom community has (1) finer sediment, (2) less oxygen in the sediment, (3) more organic matter, and (4) more deposit feeders. The sandy-bottom community has (1) larger sediment, (2) more oxygen in the sediment, (3) little organic matter, and (4) more suspension feeders.</u> The student need list only two from each.

5. (1 pt) Detritus is the primary food source in <u>unvegetated</u> soft-bottom shelf communities.

6. (1 pt) It is a <u>seagrass</u>. Algae have holdfasts.

7. (1 pt) <u>Most organisms feed on the decomposing leaves of the seagrasses.</u>

8. (1 pt) Infauna are more common in soft-bottom shelf communities and epifauna are more common in hard-bottom shelf communities. Thus, this is a hard bottom community, which is ideal for <u>algae</u>. Seagrasses need a soft bottom in which to put down roots.

9. (2 pts – one for each method) <u>Some algae can emit foul-tasting chemicals, some have leathery exteriors, and others have calcium-fortified exteriors</u>. (Any two of these is acceptable).

10. (1 pt) <u>No, you would not</u>. Kelp also need sunlight, and lots of suspended sediments would significantly reduce the light.

11. (1 pt) <u>The canopy creates more habitats up in the water column in which more organisms can live.</u>

12. (1 pt) Most likely, <u>there has been an explosion in the sea-urchin population</u>. When overpopulation causes hunger, the sea urchins eat at the holdfasts of the kelp.

13. (1 pt) <u>You would expect it to be large</u>. Since it has two chromosomes from each pair, it is diploid, which means it is from the sporophyte generation, which is the large organism we think of when we think of giant kelp. The gametophyte generation is microscopic.

Total possible points: 19

SOLUTIONS TO THE TEST FOR MODULE #13

1. (7 pts – one for each definition)

a. Epipelagic zone – The area of the water column that extends from the surface down to about 200 m

b. Meroplankton – Species of zooplankton that spend only part of their lives as members of the plankton community

c. Neuston – Planktonic organisms living at the sea surface

d. Vertical migration – Daily movement of small marine animals between the photic zone and lower depths

e. Dissolved organic matter (DOM) – Organic material dissolved in ocean water

f. Microbial loop – The flow of energy in the epipelagic beginning with the phytoplankton, dissolved organic matter, and the smallest zooplankton, making energy available to the major food web

g. Upwelling – The process that carries colder, nutrient-rich water upward to a more shallow depth

2. (1 pt) Most human activity occurs in the neritic zone of the epipelagic because it is the zone located over the continental shelf.

3. (2 pts – one for the proper characteristics of each plankton type) Holoplankton are species of zooplankton that spend their entire lives in planktonic form. Meroplankton are species of zooplankton that spend a part of their lives in planktonic form (as larvae), later changing to benthic and nektonic forms as adults.

4. (1 pt) Picoplankton feed on DOM, which would otherwise contain energy that would be lost to the ecosystem.

5. (1 pt) Copepods will most likely be the largest group collected because they are the most abundant group of zooplankton in the epipelagic zone.

6. (2 pts – one for mentioning plankton, one for mentioning mucus coverings) Larvaceans are able to capture the elusive pico-, ultra-, and nanoplankton, making the energy from their primary production available to the rest of the epipelagic. Larvaceans also produce many shed mucus coverings during their lifetime, which provides food material for epipelagic organisms as well as organisms in other zones below.

7. (1 pt) Baleen whales, whale sharks, and basking sharks are examples of large, planktivorous nektonic organisms. You need only list one.

8. (1 pt) The organism would most likely be planktonic because the projections are helpful for staying afloat by providing drag. Nektonic swimmers need to have as little drag as possible.

9. (2 pts – one for buoyancy, one for excess oxygen and higher temperatures) Swim bladders aid in buoyancy so that it is easier for these organisms to stay in the epipelagic. The dark, myoglobin-rich muscle provides excess oxygen and higher temperatures for more efficient swimming.

10. (1 pt) Violet shells prey upon members of the neuston (they are neustonic creatures as well).

11. (1 pt) These colors blend well with the filtered light penetrating the bluish water. This aids the fishes in hiding from predators.

12. (1 pt) Epipelagic zooplankton daily leave the photic zone to deeper depths to escape predation.

13. (1 pt) The microbial loop is a small food web that utilizes DOM that leaks out of the organisms that feed on it. These organisms are also a part of the major epipelagic food web, so the microbial loop is a "little web within a big web."

14. (1 pt) Because of constant wind blowing parallel to the equator and pushing surface water away, nutrient-rich deep water moves to the surface, providing materials for production. This equatorial upwelling does not occur north or south of the equator.

15. (1 pt) The weather in both places is part of a phenomenon called El Niño Southern Oscillation (ENSO), which is a see-saw effect of barometric pressure (and resulting weather) in these areas.

Total possible points: 24

SOLUTIONS TO THE TEST FOR MODULE #14

1. (5 pts – one for each definition)

a. <u>Mesopelagic zone</u> – The pelagic layer of the ocean where light can penetrate, yet without the intensity to support photosynthesis

b. <u>Photophores</u> – Organs that produce light

c. <u>Hydrothermal vent</u> – A hot, actively spreading rift zone where heated water spews up from the crust

d. <u>Bioluminescence</u> – The production of visible light by living organisms

e. <u>Chemosynthesis</u> – The making of organic material from inorganic substances using chemical energy

2. (1 pt) <u>As depth increases in the ocean, the penetration of light decreases and prevents photosynthesis from occurring</u>. This means there is less food available in deeper depths, so they can only support smaller quantities of life.

3. (1 pt) The sharp decrease in temperature indicates a thermocline. The thermometer is in the <u>mesopelagic zone</u>, because that's where the thermocline is.

4. (1 pt) The <u>pressure</u> should change more drastically. Once you get into the mesopelagic, there is so little light penetration that the temperature stays fairly constant. However, the deeper the depth, the higher the pressure, so pressure will continue to rise.

5. (1 pt) Mesopelagic fishes are <u>smaller</u> in size than their epipelagic counterparts.

6. (1 pt) <u>Because they have to wait for food to come near to them, they cannot be picky if they want to eat</u>. Therefore many mesopelagic fishes feed on practically anything they come across.

7. (3 pts – one for each feature) Fishes that vertically migrate have <u>large muscles, strong bones, and a swim bladder</u> because they have to cover great distances to get their food. They are also tolerant to drastic temperature changes.

8. (1 pt) Ventrally located photophores are helpful for camouflage because when lit, <u>they disrupt the organism's silhouette</u>, making its shape hard to discern.

9. (1 pt) The <u>presence of light</u> differentiates the mesopelagic from the deep sea. Although no photosynthesis occurs in the mesopelagic, there is some light penetration. The deep sea receives no light at all.

10. (2 pts – ½ for each chemical, and ½ for each chemical's job) A bioluminescent creature must produce <u>luciferin and luciferase. The former reacts with oxygen to produce energy in the form of light, and the latter increases the rate of the reaction.</u>

11. (1 pt) <u>It is much easier for a deep sea floor organism to find food</u>. This is because once food sinks past an individual in the water column, the food is forever lost to it. But when food lands on the sea floor, it remains there until a sea floor organism finds it.

12. (3 pts – one for each letter) a. <u>deposit feeders</u>   b. <u>bacteria</u>   c. <u>fecal pellets</u>

13. (1 pt) <u>Over time, decomposing organisms broke the dead tissue material down to a usable form for other deep sea floor organisms. Once all the carcass was fed upon, the organisms living there died</u>. While they were living there, however, they most likely reproduced, releasing their offspring into the water column to hopefully settle out onto another carcass or vent community.

Total possible points: 22

SOLUTIONS TO THE TEST FOR MODULE #15

1. (4 pts – one for each definition)

a. <u>Clupeoid fishes</u> – Small, plankton-eating fishes that travel in large schools

b. <u>Gadoid fishes</u> – Large, bottom-dwelling fishes

c. <u>Sustainable yield</u> – The amount of individuals in a population that can be caught without reducing the size of the population or letting it grow

d. <u>Mariculture</u> – The farming and harvesting of marine animals and plants

2. (1 pt) Fisheries refer to fish harvested for food as <u>finfish</u>.

3. (1 pt) Coastal upwelling <u>brings up nutrient-rich deep water, which increases primary production and supports larger populations.</u>

4. (1 pt) <u>Purse seines are used to trap large schools of clupeoid fishes.</u>

5. (1 pt) <u>Trawls are used to trap bottom-dwelling gadoid fishes.</u>

6. (1 pt) Anchoveta populations were severely decreased due to <u>overfishing</u>. (Note: In this specific case, there was another population affected. Huge populations of birds that depended on the anchoveta for food were also greatly reduced.)

7. (2 pts – one for each method) <u>Harvesting species could be regulated to only certain times of the year to avoid mating seasons. The size of harvested individuals could also be regulated to help ensure that reproduction is maximized. Only certain methods of capture could be allowed. The catch of some species could be limited. Finally, some parts of the ocean could be set aside as reserves to allow those local populations to increase.</u> The student need mention only two.

8. (1 pt) <u>Closed mariculture</u> involves controlling all aspects of an organism's environment, including water quality.

9. (1 pt) <u>Tunas are open-ocean fishes that require habitats that cannot be reproduced in a mariculture setting.</u>

10. (2 pts – one for the definition, one for an example) A renewable resource is a <u>resource that can naturally replace harvested numbers.</u> Some examples of renewable marine resources are <u>seaweeds, shellfish such as oysters, and finfish such as tunas.</u> Basically, the student can list any living resource.

11. (1 pt) <u>Reverse osmosis does not produce a residue of salts, and it takes less energy than distillation.</u>

12. (1 pt) <u>The structures are used to harness the mechanical energy of currents or waves in order to convert it to electrical energy.</u>

Total possible points: 17

SOLUTIONS TO THE TEST FOR MODULE #16

1. (4 pts – one for each definition)

a. <u>Eutrophication</u> – Excessive algal growth as a result of increased nutrient input

b. <u>Nonbiodegradable</u> – Substances that cannot be broken down by bacteria or other organisms

c. <u>Biomagnification</u> – The increasing concentration of a substance from one trophic level to the next

d. <u>Fouling organisms</u> – Organisms that live attached to surfaces that are under water, causing negative effects to ships and pilings

2. (2 pts – one for the indirect processes and one for the direct processes. Take 2/5 off for each wrongly identified process) <u>Letters (b) and (e) are activities that indirectly affect the estuary</u>, since they do not alter the estuary immediately. <u>Letters (a), (c), and (d) are activities that directly affect the estuary</u>, as they have an immediate effect.

3. (1 pt) <u>Cyanide can kill the coral reef or cause it to bleach</u> (throw off its symbiotic algae), severely reducing its survivability. The student need give only one possibility.

4. (1 pt) <u>After treatment, there is usually residual chlorine present in the sewage, which is as detrimental to the ocean as untreated sewage.</u>

5. (1 pt) Once sewage is initially treated by chlorine or ozone it is sent to settling tanks and becomes sludge (primary treatment). Sludge is very similar to marine detritus. <u>When it is dumped into marshes, the bacteria in the mud break down the organic matter and make the nutrients bound up in the sludge available to the plants in the marsh. This represents a secondary treatment of the sewage.</u>

6. (1 pt) It probably has <u>strong waves</u> and tidal actions, which aid in oil removal.

7. (1 pt) <u>The deep-ocean seafloor most likely has naturally produced oil pollution.</u> Deep ocean seeps are the major natural way that oil gets into the ocean.

8. (1 pt) <u>You would expect to find larger quantities of the nonbiodegradable chemical in the marine mammals.</u> If a chemical is biodegradable, it gets broken down and does not accumulate strongly in the fat tissue of organisms. As a result, it will not be magnified as it travels up the trophic pyramid. The nonbiodegrable one will be subject to biomagnification, so it will get more concentrated as it travels up the trophic pyramid.

9. (1 pt) <u>Heavy metals such as lead and mercury are also subject to biomagnification</u>, because they are stored in fat cells and do not biodegrade. The student can say either "heavy metals" or name either lead or mercury to get credit. Give the student half credit if he indicates that any fat-soluble, nonbiodegradable substance is subject to biomagnification.

10. (1 pt) <u>Radioactive waste</u> does not have to be eaten to affect an organism, and it is harmful to nearly all living things.

11. (1 pt) <u>Small bits of Styrofoam may be viewed as morsels of food for smaller fish</u>. If they eat them, they can have all sorts of digestive problems, potentially leading to death.

12. (1 pt) <u>The rubble will provide a hard substrate for coral, perhaps making the beginning of a lush, beautiful coral reef</u>.

Total possible points: 16

QUARTERLY TEST #1

1. You are shown two samples of the earth's crust. The first is more dense than the second. Which, most likely, is oceanic crust?

2. Although the temperature of the air above the ocean can change dramatically, the temperature of the water in the ocean does not change nearly as dramatically. Why?

3. You are making a light detector that you will lower into the ocean. You want it to detect light as deep in the water as possible. The detector must be set up to detect a range of wavelengths that correspond to one of the colors of the rainbow. Which color should you set the detector to sense?

4. Suppose the earth rotated opposite of the direction it currently rotates. What effect would that have on the directions of the ocean gyres?

5. If you stay on the beach for 24 hours straight, how many high tides will you experience?

6. As you lower a thermometer into the ocean, you notice a slow, steady decrease in temperature. Suddenly, however, the temperature decreases *very* quickly. What has the thermometer just passed through?

7. The salinity of the fluids in a marine organism's body changes when the salinity of the water around it changes. Is the organism a osmoregulator or an osmoconformer?

8. Suppose you study a salt water aquarium that contains only producers (no consumers). In addition, there are no air pumps or bubblers adding air to the water. The aquarium is simulating a natural tide pool. Suppose you are monitoring the carbon dioxide concentration in the water on an hourly basis. When the lights are off for a while, will the carbon dioxide level fall, rise, or stay the same?

9. Order these levels of biological organization by increasing size. Start with the smallest, and end with the largest:

   cell, organism, atom, community, tissue, molecule, ecosystem, cellular organelle, organ, population

10. An organism's body temperature varies with the outside temperature, but it is generally several degrees higher than the outside temperature. Is this organism homeotherm or a poikilotherm? Is it an ectotherm or an endotherm?

11. You are examining the gametes produced by a marine organism. Each gamete has 20 chromosomes. If you examine the skin cells from this organism, how many chromosomes will it have?

12. In marine waters with little sunlight, would you expect to find a large population of heterotrophs?

13. A student refers to a certain microscopic organism as "blue-green algae." Although the student is correct, what is a better name for the organism?

14. Describe the one sexual and two asexual modes of reproduction in diatoms.

15. You are looking at a dinoflagellate and see only one flagellum extending from the back of the cell. Where is the other one?

16. A seaweed has four basic parts: the holdfast, pneumatocysts, and what two others?

17. A seaweed reproduces using the alternation of generations type of life cycle, and its thallus is presently in the diploid sporophyte generation. What will the organism in this generation produce for reproduction? Will it generate this by mitosis or meiosis?

18. A lichen represents a symbiosis between what two types of organisms?

19. Of what specific type of symbiosis is a lichen an example?

20. Are the larvae of sponges stationary like the adults?

21. What specialized cells move water through a sponge and trap its food?

22. If a cnidarian is not in a medusa form, which form must it be in?

23. Are all plankton microscopic?

24. Many corals have a mutualistic relationship with what microorganism?

25. The body wall of an organism is very thin. Does it most likely have gills? Why or why not?

QUARTERLY TEST #2

1. Give an example of each of the following: a gastropod, a bivalve, and a cephalopod.

2. An organism's blood never comes into direct contact with its tissues. Does it have an open or closed circulatory system?

3. What is the sheath of tissue surrounding the internal organs of a mollusk called?

4. What must an arthropod do regularly in order to grow?

5. A sea star can only open a clam slightly, because the clam has strong muscles that hold its shell closed. How does a sea star eat a clam?

6. Why are lancelets and tunicates placed in phylum Chordata even though they are technically invertebrates?

7. An adult lamprey is caught in fresh water. What is it most likely doing there?

8. When viewed under a microscope, the skeleton of a fish has no osteocytes. Is it a shark or a bony fish?

9. What is the name of the fin that is on the very end of the shark's body?

10. What do most rays have instead of teeth?

11. A fish has a tapered body shape. Is it a fast-moving predator, a demersal fish, a slow-moving reef-swimmer, or does it live in narrow crevices of rock and coral?

12. How can fishes "feel" the presence of things in the water?

13. Why do fishes school?

14. What is the purpose of the salt gland in sea turtles?

15. If you find a healthy female sea turtle on shore, what is she most likely doing?

16. If you are looking at a bird bone that is about as heavy as a dog bone of similar size, from what type of bird did it most likely come?

17. What is baleen, and how does a whale use it?

18. What role does a dolphin's melon play in echolocation?

19. Why do some marine mammals experience delayed implantation?

20. How can a predator use camouflage to catch prey?

21. Identify the organisms in the food web below that feed as secondary consumers at least some of the time:

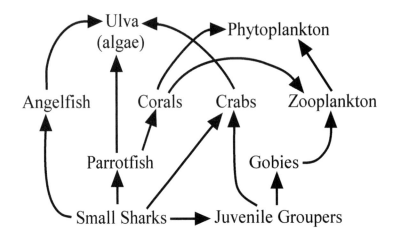

22. Name the two techniques used for measuring productivity in a marine ecosystem, and indicate which is the better technique.

23. In the carbon cycle, do the decomposers increase or decrease the amount of carbon dioxide in the water?

24. If you were measuring the amount of nitrogen gas in an enclosed ecosystem and someone suddenly added a lot of nitrogen-fixing bacteria to the ecosystem, would the nitrogen gas levels increase or decrease?

25. If a benthic organism is always under water but is never exposed to light, does it live in the splash zone, the intertidal zone, the inner shelf, or the outer shelf of the ocean?

QUARTERLY TEST #3

1. You are measuring the temperature and salinity in a tide pool during low tide. If it is a nice, sunny day, what will most likely happen to your measurements as the day progresses?

2. When a limpet seals itself against a rock to trap moisture, what is it trying to avoid? Use the technical term.

3. Do organisms in the lower areas of the intertidal zone have an easier or harder time feeding than organisms living in the upper areas?

4. What are byssal threads, and what organisms produce them?

5. What types of factors (abiotic or biotic) determine the upper limit of living space for an intertidal organism? What about the lower limit?

6. If a zone in the rocky intertidal has an amazing variety of organisms, is it most likely the upper, middle, or lower intertidal?

7. If you are looking for a wide variety of organisms buried in the substrate of a muddy intertidal area, should you look near the surface or deep in the mud?

8. According to most scientists, during what period or periods in earth's history were most estuaries formed?

9. A sessile organism is living at a given point on the substrate of an estuary. How does the salinity that it experiences change from low tide to high tide?

10. In an estuary, a stenohaline salt water organism can survive further inland along the right side of the river (as you float on the ocean and look back to the coast) than on the left. Is this estuary in the Northern or Southern Hemisphere?

11. Which organisms (euryhaline, stenohaline, or brackish water) tend to live well in all areas of an estuary?

12. A scientist is studying a wetland with a mangrove forest. Is this a temperate or tropical area?

13. Which type of mangrove has salt glands?

14. Which are more common in mudflats: deposit feeders or filter feeders?

15. Coral growth requires warm water and what other two things?

16. In a coral community, the individual polyps are often connected by a thin layer of tissue. What is this layer of tissue called?

17. Name two ways that coral can asexually reproduce.

18. Corals can trap plankton or extend filaments to catch food particles. What is the other method by which corals get food?

19. What is the most likely explanation for the formation of atolls?

20. A coral has spicules. Is it a stony coral or a soft coral?

21. Identify the following organisms as benthos, nekton, or plankton: larval fish, tuna, lobster, stingray, manta ray, jellyfish.

22. You are studying a soft-bottom shelf community in the tropics. If it is vegetated, what type of seagrass will you find there?

23. Do most organisms that feed on seagrass eat it while it is alive or after it has died?

24. Where would you find more seaweeds: in a hard-bottom shelf community or a soft-bottom shelf community?

25. You are looking at non-reproductive cells from two different individual kelps of the same species. Despite the fact that they are from individuals of the same species, the cells have different numbers of chromosomes. How can this be?

QUARTERLY TEST #4

1. When an epipelagic organism dies and sinks to the deep ocean, nutrients have passed from the epipelagic zone to the deeper zones. What is another way that nutrients can travel from the epipelagic zone to the deep ocean?

2. What organisms feed on dissolved organic matter (DOM)?

3. Distinguish between holoplankton and meroplankton.

4. Fill in the blank: Some creatures stay afloat in the epipelagic by creating drag. Others stay afloat in the epipelagic by creating _____.

5. Most fishes in the epipelagic have a dorsal surface that is darkly colored and a ventral surface that is silvery white. What is the technical term for this type of camouflage?

6. How do overturn and upwelling affect primary production in the epipelagic?

7. Is primary production in the epipelagic generally high or low along the coasts?

8. Does any light make it into the mesopelagic zone?

9. Most mesopelagic fishes will eat nearly anything they can find. Why?

10. A mesopelagic fish has watery flesh and little muscle tone. It also has no swim bladder. Does this fish use vertical migration or a sit-and-wait strategy to find food?

11. Besides black, which color is very hard to see in the mesopelagic?

12. You have two lights of similar intensity. One is a standard light bulb, the other uses a process similar to bioluminescence. Which will be warmer to the touch?

13. Name one strategy that deep sea organisms use to help increase their likelihood of mating.

14. Is there any photosynthesis taking place in the deep sea?

15. Which group of marine organisms are more heavily harvested for food: finfish or shellfish?

16. What are clupeoid fishes?

17. How is a purse seine used to catch fishes?

18. Why should the goal be to catch the maximum sustainable yield for each population that is fished?

19. How can good marketing help manage fish populations in the ocean?

20. What is the difference between open mariculture and closed mariculture?

21. What is desalinization?

22. What is coral bleaching, and what does it indicate?

23. What is eutrophication?

24. Trace amounts of a fat-soluble, nonbiodegradable chemical are found in the phytoplankton of a marine ecosystem. Do you expect to find trace amounts or large amounts of the chemical in the marine mammals of the ecosystem?

25. What are fouling organisms, and why is it beneficial to the environment to keep them off ship hulls?

SOLUTIONS TO QUARTERLY TEST #1

1. (1 pt) The <u>first</u> is oceanic crust, because oceanic crust is more dense than continental crust, which is why it floats lower in the mantle.

2. (1 pt) <u>Water has a very large specific heat</u>, which means that it takes a lot of energy to change its temperature.

3. (1 pt) You should set it to sense <u>blue</u> light, since blue light penetrates water the deepest.

4. (1 pt) <u>The gyres would flow in the opposite directions</u>, because the winds would be bent in the opposite directions. Thus, the Northern Hemisphere gyres would be counterclockwise, while the Southern Hemisphere gyres would be clockwise.

5. (1 pt) You will experience <u>two</u> high tides and two low tides. This is true in *most* parts of the world. There are a few locations that experience only one tidal change during certain seasons.

6. (1 pt) It has just passed through the <u>thermocline</u>, which separates the warm, shallow waters and the cold, deep waters.

7. (1 pt) It is an <u>osmoconformer</u>. Osmoregulators have mechanisms that keep the salinity of their body fluids the same regardless of the salinity of their surroundings.

8. (1 pt) It will <u>rise</u>. When the lights are off, the producers cannot do photosynthesis, which uses up carbon dioxide. However, they will still do respiration, which makes carbon dioxide. As a result, carbon dioxide will be added to the water but not used up.

9. (2 pts – 1/5 for each answer in the proper order) <u>atom, molecule, cellular organelle, cell, tissue, organ, organism, population, community, ecosystem</u>

10. (2 pts – 1 for each answer) It is a <u>poikilotherm</u> and an <u>endotherm</u>.

11. (1 pt) Gametes are haploid cells, which means they have half the number of chromosomes as the rest of the cells in the body. Thus, the skin cells will have <u>40</u> chromosomes.

12. (1 pt) <u>No</u>. If there is little sunlight, there will be few producers. As a result, there will be little upon which heterotrophs can feed.

13. (1 pt) The proper name is <u>cyanobacteria</u>. Algae are eukaryotic, but blue-green algae are not. Thus, it is best to not call them algae. Since they are prokaryotic, it is best to call them bacteria.

14. (3 pts – 1 for each mode) <u>Asexual modes: splitting their frustules</u> and <u>shedding their frustules to form an auxospore</u>. <u>Sexual mode: forming gametes that make an auxospore after fertilization</u>.

15. (1 pt) The other flagellum is <u>wrapped in a groove that goes around the middle of the cell</u>.

16. (2 pts – 1 for each part) The other two parts are the <u>stipe</u> and <u>blades</u>.

17. (2 pts – 1 for each answer) Since it is in its sporophyte generation, it will produce <u>spores</u> to reproduce. Since it is diploid, however, in order to make the next generation haploid (that's what alternation of generation does), it will have to produce these spores by <u>meiosis</u>.

18. (2 pts – 1 for each organism) A lichen is a symbiotic relationship between an <u>alga</u> and a <u>fungus</u>.

19. (1 pt) It is an example of <u>mutualism</u>, because each organism benefits from the other.

20. (1 pt) <u>No</u>. The larvae of sponges are planktonic so that they can be transported to a new place upon which to grow.

21. (1 pt) <u>Collar cells</u> perform these functions.

22. (1 pt) It must be in a <u>polyp</u> form, as that is the only other possible form for a cnidarian.

23. (1 pt) <u>No</u>. Plankton are those organisms that cannot swim against the currents. Since most jellyfish cannot swim against the currents, they are plankton, even though they are not microscopic.

24. (1 pt) Many corals have a mutualistic relationship with <u>zooxanthellae</u>.

25. (2 pts – 1 for no, and 1 for why not) <u>No. Since the body wall is thin, oxygen can diffuse right into the body, and carbon dioxide can diffuse right out</u>.

Total possible points: 33

SOLUTIONS TO QUARTERLY TEST #2

1. (3 pts – 1 for each example) The gastropods include <u>snails, abalones, and limpets</u>. The bivalves include <u>clams, oysters, and scallops</u>. The cephalopods include <u>octopuses, squids, and cuttlefish</u>. The student should give only one for each group.

2. (1 pt) It has a <u>closed circulatory system</u>. In an open circulatory system, the tissues are bathed in blood.

3. (1 pt) It is called the <u>mantle</u>.

4. (1 pt) It must <u>molt</u>.

5. (1 pt) <u>A sea star can evert its stomach</u>, which means it pushes its stomach out of its body and slips its stomach inside the tiny opening for feeding.

6. (1 pt) They are put in phylum Chordata because <u>they have a notochord in at least some point of their development</u>. In vertebrates, the notochord develops into a vertebral column. In lancelets, it stays throughout the organism's life, but it never develops into a vertebral column. In the tunicates, it actually degenerates as the larva turns into an adult.

7. (1 pt) It is most likely <u>reproducing</u>, because lampreys live in the ocean for most of their adult lives and return to fresh water only to reproduce.

8. (1 pt) It is a <u>shark</u>. If it were a bony fish, it would have to have calcified bones, which contain osteocytes.

9. (1 pt) That is the <u>caudal fin</u>.

10. (1 pt) They have <u>dental plates</u> that crush their food.

11. (1 pt) It is a <u>fast-moving predator</u>, because the tapered body shape allows it to swim very quickly.

12. (1 pt) They have a <u>lateral line</u> along their bodies that is sensitive to vibrations and pressure changes in the water.

13. (1 pt – either answer is fine) Fishes may school for the <u>protection</u> a group would provide. Others may school to help <u>round up prey while feeding</u>.

14. (1 pt) It helps them <u>remove excess salt from their body fluids</u>.

15. (1 pt) She is most likely <u>laying eggs</u>. That's the only reason they come to shore.

16. (1 pt) It most likely came from a <u>penguin</u>, because they have dense bones that help them sink in the water.

17. (2 pts – 1 for what it is, and one for how it is used) Baleen consists of <u>rows of comb-like horny plates that project from the upper jaws of certain whales</u>. It is used to <u>filter plankton from the water, which the whale eats</u>.

18. (1 pt) The melon <u>focuses and directs the clicks</u> that the dolphin makes for echolocation.

19. (1 pt) Since the migratory marine mammals get to their breeding grounds once a year, they need to carry their embryo for a full year. Delayed implantation occurs specifically <u>to lengthen gestation periods that are shorter than one year so that the calf will be born at the breeding grounds</u>.

20. (1 pt) The predator can <u>blend in so well with the surroundings that the prey doesn't even see the predator and therefore doesn't know to avoid it</u>.

21. (5 pts – 1 for each organism) <u>Corals, gobies, juvenile groupers, small sharks, and parrotfish</u> feed as secondary consumers at least part of the time.

22. (3 pts – 1 for each technique, and one for which is better) The two techniques are the <u>light and dark bottle technique</u> and the <u>radioactive carbon technique</u>. The <u>radioactive carbon technique is better</u>.

23. (1 pt) Decomposition <u>increases</u> the amount of carbon dioxide in the water.

24. (1 pt) They would <u>decrease</u>, because nitrogen fixation converts nitrogen gas into nitrates, nitrites, and ammonia.

25. (1 pt) Since it never experiences light, it is in the aphotic zone. The only one of those listed that is in the aphotic zone is the <u>outer shelf</u>.

Total Possible Points: 34

SOLUTIONS TO QUARTERLY TEST #3

1. (2 pts – 1 for each effect) The temperature will <u>increase</u> as the sun heats the water, and the salinity will <u>increase</u> as the water evaporates.

2. (1 pt – if the student describes it but does not give the technical term, give ½ point) The limpet is trying to avoid <u>dessication</u>, which means to become dried out.

3. (1 pt) Organisms in the lower portion of the intertidal zone have an <u>easier</u> time feeding because they are covered with water more, and water brings in food.

4. (2 pts – 1 for what they are and 1 for what organisms produce them) Byssal threads are <u>strands of proteins that harden to attach the organism to a substrate</u>. <u>Mussels produce them</u>.

5. (2 pts – 1 for the upper limit and 1 for the lower limit) <u>The upper limit of living space is determined by abiotic factors</u>, such as salinity, temperature, and moisture availability. <u>The lower limit of living space is determined by biotic factors</u>, such as predation and competition among individuals for space.

6. (1 pt) It is most likely the <u>lower intertidal</u>, because it is under water the longest and therefore can support more marine life.

7. (1 pt) You should look <u>near the surface</u>. Since water doesn't seep through mud well, the lower depths are anaerobic. Organisms live near the surface to get access to oxygen.

8. (1 pt) Most scientists think that estuaries formed during an <u>ice age</u>. They differ on how many ice ages there were, however.

9. (1 pt) The salinity will continually <u>increase</u> as the tide brings in seawater.

10. (1 pt) Since it is a stenohaline creature, it needs high salinities. This means the right side of the river is higher in salinity. When looking at the river as described, the gyres make the left side of the river higher in salinity in the Northern Hemisphere and the right side higher in salinity in the <u>Southern Hemisphere</u>.

11. (1 pt) <u>Euryhaline</u> species can tolerate a wide range of salinities and therefore can live well in most areas of an estuary.

12. (1 pt) Mangrove forests are typically found in <u>tropical</u> wetlands.

13. (1 pt) <u>White mangroves</u> have salt glands.

14. (1 pt) <u>Deposit feeders</u> are more common. The high levels of suspended sediments in mudflats clog up filter feeding apparati.

15. (2 pts – 1 for each answer) Coral growth also requires a <u>hard substrate</u> and <u>sunlight</u>.

16. (1 pt) The thin layer of tissue connecting polyps is called a <u>coenosarc</u>.

17. (2 pts – 1 for each method) <u>Coral can asexually reproduce upwards by moving up and secreting an elevated bottom and extended sides of the corallite. Coral can also grow laterally by budding off a portion of their body and secreting a new corallite. And finally, a new coral colony can begin when a piece of existing live coral is broken off</u>. The student need list only two.

18. (1 pt) Coral also get food from the <u>photosynthesis of the zooxanthellae</u>.

19. (3 pts – 1 point for each stage) Stage 1: <u>Atolls probably started out as fringing reefs around a volcano that was jutting above the water</u>. Stage 2: <u>As the waters rose or the volcano sunk (or both), the fringing reef rose to the point that it became a barrier reef, with the tip of the volcano at the center</u>. Stage 3: <u>As the waters rose or the volcano sunk even more, eventually the volcano was no longer above the water, and the barrier reef became an atoll</u>.

20. (1 pt) Only a <u>soft coral</u> produces spicules.

21. (3 pts – ½ for each) Larval fish: <u>plankton</u>. Tuna: <u>nekton</u>. Lobster: <u>benthos</u>. Stingray: <u>benthos</u>. Manta ray: <u>nekton</u>. Jellyfish: <u>plankton</u>

22. (1 pt) You will find <u>turtle grass</u> there.

23. (1 pt) Although there are exceptions, most organisms that feed on seagrass feed on it <u>after it is dead</u> and decaying.

24. (1 pt) Seaweeds need a hard substrate on which to attach, so they are more plentiful in <u>hard-bottom shelf communities</u>.

25. (1 pt) <u>You are looking at a cell from an individual in the gametophyte generation and a cell from an individual in the sporophyte generation</u>. Since kelps follow an alternation of generations life cycle, one generation will be diploid, while the next is haploid. As a result, the cells from individuals in different generations will have different numbers of chromosomes.

Total Possible Points: 34

SOLUTIONS TO QUARTERLY TEST #4

1. (1 pt) <u>An epipelagic fish can swim into the deeper parts of the ocean and get eaten</u>. Alternatively, the student could mention vertical migration, in which organisms from the deeper zone rise to eat epipelagic organisms.

2. (1 pt) The tiniest organisms, <u>ultraplankton, nanoplankton, and picoplankton</u> feed on DOM. The student need list only one.

3. (1 pt) <u>Holoplankton spend their entire lives as plankton, while meroplankton are only plankton for part of their lives</u>.

4. (1 pt) Some creatures stay afloat in the epipelagic by creating drag. Others stay afloat in the epipelagic by creating <u>buoyancy</u>.

5. (1 pt) It is called <u>countershading</u>.

6. (1 pt) These processes bring nutrient-rich deep water into the epipelagic waters, <u>greatly increasing primary production</u>.

7. (1 pt) Primary production is generally <u>high</u> along the coasts because the winds and waves result in constant nutrient mixing.

8. (1 pt) <u>Yes</u>. In general the mesopelagic has enough light for creatures to see one another, but not enough light for photosynthesis.

9. (1 pt) <u>The scarcity of food</u> in the mesopelagic requires the fishes to have broad eating habits.

10. (1 pt) It must use a <u>sit-and-wait</u> strategy, because it does not have the features of a vertical migrator.

11. (1 pt) <u>Red</u> is hard to see in the mesopelagic, because red light does not penetrate deeply into the water column.

12. (1 pt) <u>The standard light bulb</u> will be warmer to the touch, because a lot more of its energy is converted to heat instead of light.

13. (1 pt) Some fishes are <u>hermaphroditic</u> so that they can mate with *any* other member of the same species. Other fishes employ <u>male parasitism</u>, where the male latches onto the female for life. The student need list only one.

14. (1 pt) <u>Yes</u>. There are some species that do photosynthesis from the blackbody radiation that comes from hydrothermal vents.

15. (1 pt) <u>Finfish</u> are the most harvested for food.

16. (2 pts – 1 for small, the other for schools) They are <u>small, plankton-eating fishes that travel in large schools</u>.

17. (1 pt) A purse seine is a long, flat net with weights along the bottom edge and floats along the top. The net encircles a school of fish, and then the weighted end is drawn up, trapping the fish inside.

18. (1 pt) Catching the maximum sustainable yield will produce the most food without adversely affecting the population.

19. (1 pt) Marketing can convince people to eat marine creatures they would not normally think of eating. This can reduce the demand for a species that has a dwindling population, replacing it with demand for a species that is plentiful.

20. (2 pts – 1 for each type of mariculture) In open mariculture, the fish are raised in an enclosed portion of an existing marine environment. As a result, the environment is controlled by natural forces. In closed mariculture, the fish are raised in a completely artificial setting where the environment is completely controlled.

21. (1 pt) It is the process by which salt is removed from seawater to make fresh water, which is usually used for drinking.

22. (2 pts – 1 for what it is and 1 for what it indicates) Bleaching is when corals spontaneously throw off a majority of their symbiotic zooxanthellae, resulting in a whitish color on their surface. It is an indication that the coral is under stress and vulnerable to disease. The student need not mention vulnerable to disease. Mentioning stress is good enough.

23. (1 pt) It is excessive algal growth as a result of increased nutrient input.

24. (1 pt) You expect to find large amounts due to biomagnification.

25. (2 pts – 1 for what they are and 1 for why they need to be kept off ship hulls) They are organisms that live attached to surfaces that are underwater, causing negative effects to ships and pilings. They need to be kept off ship hulls because they increase drag, which causes the ships to use more energy to travel. The more energy you use, the more you must make, which results in more pollution.

Total Possible Points: 29

TEST FOR MODULE #1

1. Define the following terms:

a. Oceanic crust
b. Continental crust
c. Mid-ocean ridge
d. Subduction
e. Salinity
f. Coriolis effect
g. Gyres

2. If an organism had sufficient energy (and time) and had no restrictions on its temperature, salinity or food requirements, could it conceivably travel through all four major ocean basins of the world? Why or why not?

3. Why is oceanic crust under water, while continental crust is not?

4. How is new sea floor created?

5. Why is there more life in the continental shelf region of the ocean than in the abyssal plain?

6. Name one benefit hydrogen bonding provides for marine organisms.

7. How do salinity and temperature affect the density of water?

8. Along a certain fictitious seashore, there is a processing plant that dumps its byproducts of sand and clay into the ocean. Assuming everything else is the same along this shore, would you expect more or less life near the processing plant? Why?

9. All the major currents of the ocean are driven by what phenomenon?

10. Why is the average surface temperature of the ocean near the coast of Portugal much colder than the average surface temperature of North Carolina even though they are at similar latitudes?

11. What is the difference between a spring tide and a neap tide? What causes this difference?

12. If an organism is in the deep layer of the ocean, what feature of the vertical parts of the ocean would it have to cross in order to get to the warmer surface layer above it?

TEST FOR MODULE #2

1. Define the following terms:

a. Autotrophs
b. Heterotrophs
c. Respiration
d. Homeostasis
e. Poikilotherm
f. Homeotherm
g. Binomial nomenclature

2. What are the four major groups of organic molecules involved in the metabolic process?

3. Suppose the population of marine algae in Creation increased dramatically. What would most likely happen to the levels of oxygen and carbon dioxide in the atmosphere?

4. As you will learn in a later module, there are organisms down in the very deep parts of the ocean where light cannot penetrate. These organisms, however, can produce their own energy from various chemicals in their environment. Would you classify these individuals as autotrophs or heterotrophs?

5. If a single-celled organism can propel itself through the water, can you tell if it is a prokaryote or a eukaryote just by this information?

6. Distinguish between an organ and a tissue.

7. Which part of a cell allows only selected molecules to enter inside?

8. Tide pools are areas at the shoreline of oceans that sometimes become isolated from the waves and thus are exposed to the sun's heat, evaporation, or rain. If an osmoregulator found itself in such a tide pool, would the composition of its body fluids change with the changing tide pool conditions?

9. Explain how a large tuna can remain active in cold water despite the fact that its body temperature changes with its environment.

10. Corals are organisms that can reproduce both asexually by individuals dividing into two identical individuals, or sexually by broadcasting gametes into the water. If you come across a colony of coral that is connected together, is it more likely that the individuals in this colony are a result of asexual reproduction or sexual reproduction?

11. Two marine organisms appear to be very similar and are bred together in an aquarium, producing offspring. The aquarium owner tries to breed the next generation a year later in order to sell their offspring, but they do not appear to be fertile. Assuming there is no problem with the water quality or nutrition, what could you suppose about the first two organisms?

TEST FOR MODULE #3

1. Define the following terms:

a. Bacteria
b. Decomposers
c. Phytoplankton
d. Zooplankton
e. Thallus
f. Haploid
g. Diploid
h. Symbiosis

2. What are two processes that autotrophic bacteria can use to convert energy into organic matter?

3. Why aren't cyanobacteria considered algae?

4. List two ways diatoms benefit humans.

5. While hiking, you find a large amount of abrasive, whitish powder on the side of a mountain. Your guide says it is made up of tiny fossilized bits of silica. How do you know that this area was probably once under the ocean?

6. Why won't some restaurants serve fish harvested in areas of planktonic blooms?

7. What is the function of the pneumatocysts on a thallus?

8. Which type of algae (green, brown, or red) provides merchants with the emulsifying agent called algin? What does algin do?

9. A seaweed that follows the alternation of generations life cycle produces haploid (1n) spores. Into what type of generation will those haploid spores develop: sporophyte or gametophyte? Will that new generation be haploid or diploid?

10. What two types of organisms are associated with one another in a lichen?

11. Why don't the seagrasses need large, showy flowers?

12. What part of the red mangrove can help to accumulate sediment buildup?

TEST FOR MODULE #4

1. Define the following terms:

a. Amoebocytes
b. Metamorphosis
c. Polyp
d. Medusa

e. Mesoglea
f. Mutualism
g. Commensalism
h. Parasitism

2. Give one example each of a marine organism that exhibits (1) radial symmetry and (2) bilateral symmetry.

3. What are the two possible forms of support in sponges?

4. Despite the fact that polyps are generally stationary, cnidarians with only a polyp form can spread to populate vast regions of the ocean. How do they accomplish this without moving?

5. Give at least three features common to cnidarians in both the polyp and medusa stages.

6. Which of the three classes of phylum Cnidaria is composed of organisms spending most, if not all, of their life cycle as a large medusa form: the Hydrozoa, the Scyphozoa, or the Anthozoa?

7. A coral reef is a colony of anthozoan polyps. What part of it is actually alive?

8. An organism has a brain. Is it most likely bilaterally symmetric or radially symmetric?

9. A worm has no gut. Of the worms we studied in this module, which kind is it?

10. Give an example of a parasite from this module.

11. An organism is described as having a definite head and rear end; its long, thin body is made up of a series of similar compartments; and it has a definite, fluid-filled coelom. In what phylum would you classify this animal?

12. The lophophorates are grouped together because all the organisms have a lophophore. What is this structure, and what does it do?

TEST FOR MODULE #5

1. Define the following terms:

a. Mantle   e. Cephalothorax
b. Radula   f. Carapace
c. Chitin   g. Ambulacral groove
d. Molting   h. Dorsal nerve cord

2. The organisms in the phylum Mollusca have a diverse array of body forms. What are two basic body parts that most members of this group have in common?

3. Give an example of a gastropod, an example of a bivalve, and an example of a cephalopod.

4. Identify the structures in the clam illustration below:

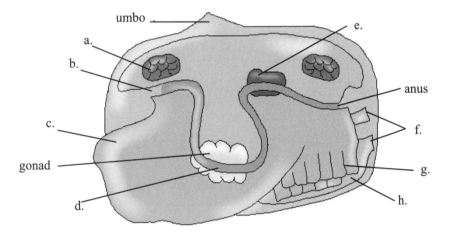

5. In an aquarium, you find what appears to be a shrimp sitting among the plants and rocks, yet when you reach in to pick it up, you find that it is just an outer covering that is completely hollow. What must have happened?

6. Cleaner shrimp display the symbiosis of mutualism in the ocean. Explain this relationship and with what organisms the shrimp are involved.

7. Explain how most female crustaceans can hatch multiple batches of fertilized eggs even though they may not be near males often.

8. What is the importance of the water vascular system in the echinoderms?

9. At a marine aquarium tide pool tank, some children are taking turns holding a sea cucumber. They begin to play with it rather roughly, and suddenly a large amount of material is squirted out of the sea cucumber's body. What happened? Is the sea cucumber hurt?

10. Explain why sea cucumbers and sea urchins need long, coiled guts.

11. A biologist is examining some recently collected marine water under a microscope and notices some echinoderm gametes. She reasons that she had better study them closely now, because it will probably be a while before water from the same region will once again contain such gametes. Why is her reasoning likely to be correct?

12. What is the function of a notochord? Adult tunicates do not have a notochord. What feature performs the notochord's function in the adults?

13. Give two examples of organisms that are in phylum Chordata but are invertebrates.

14. In which phylum do you find each of the following and what is its function?

       a. radula   b. exoskeleton   c. water vascular system   d. notochord

TEST FOR MODULE #6

1. Define the following terms:

a. Demersal
b. Chromatophores
c. Hermaphroditism
d. Oviparous
e. Viviparous

2. The members of class Agnatha are characterized by features they do not have. Name two of those features.

3. Some birds and marine mammals are considered by scientists to be very "advanced" because of their remarkable ability to migrate from one area of the world to the other without ever having been shown the way. How could you refute this statement using the lampreys as an example?

4. A fish has a jaw, but its skeleton contains no osteocytes or osteoblasts. Is it a lamprey, a ray, or a bony fish?

5. The design of rays is perfect for their demersal life style. Name two characteristics helpful to these fish.

6. What *external* feature on a bony fish ensures that the water flows across the gills so as to maximize the amount of oxygen that gets into the capillaries of the gills?

7. What special feature does a bony fish have that aids in its ability to rise in the water column?

8. Name at least three physical features of a bony fish that distinguish it from a cartilaginous fish.

9. A fish has a large, dark spot near its tail. Is this an example of camouflage, disguise, or advertisement?

10. Explain the purpose of the spiral intestine in sharks.

11. What is the name for the specialized system of blood flow in the gills of fishes?

12. What are the lateral line and ampullae of Lorenzini in sharks?

13. Explain the difference between anadromous behavior and catadromous behavior in fishes.

14. A certain fish produces only a few eggs for fertilization. Is this fish most likely oviparous or ovoviviparous?

(The test is continued on the next page.)

15. Identify the structures pointed out in the diagram below:

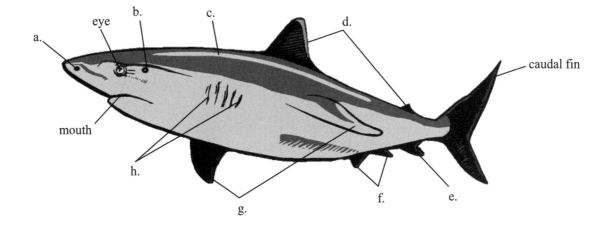

TEST FOR MODULE #7

1. Define the following terms:

a. Adaptation
b. Baleen
c. Echolocation
d. Behavior
e. Delayed implantation

2. During the time of year when sea turtle eggs hatch, the population of predatory birds near the shoreline tends to increase. Why?

3. What does the salt gland do for marine birds?

4. How is the adaptation of a laterally flattened tail helpful to marine iguanas and sea snakes?

5. Where are you more likely to find marine reptiles: warmer or colder climates?

6. Pelicans and terns both dive into the water to catch their prey. Pelicans are better swimmers, however. Why?

7. A person finds a very large jawbone washed up on the beach. It is so large that it must be from a whale. How can the person tell if it was from a baleen whale or not?

8. The largest animals on earth, the baleen whales, feed on the tiniest of organisms, the plankton. How can a diet of such small organisms be beneficial to support such huge organisms?

9. Which marine mammal order contains animals that spend their entire lives in the water: Sirenia, Pinnipedia, or Carnivora?

10. Would you expect to find a melon on a toothed whale or a baleen whale?

11. Consider the echolocation system of a dolphin. Explain how the clicks are generated in the dolphin, as well as how the echoes are received and processed. Include the major anatomical structures related to the echolocation system in your answer.

12. Why do dolphins not get the bends when they dive deeply?

13. You see what might be a seal or a sea lion swimming in the water. What can you look for to determine whether it is a seal or a sea lion?

14. What detail of cetacean birth minimizes the risk of the calf drowning?

15. A migratory marine mammal does not experience delayed implantation. What is the approximate gestation period for its young?

TEST FOR MODULE #8

1. Define the following terms:

a. Ecology   e. Limiting resource
b. Abiotic   f. Detritus
c. Biotic   g. Productivity
d. Carrying capacity   h. Carbon fixation

2. A certain species of fish feeds exclusively on green macroalgae within an ecosystem. Suppose there was a drastic change in an abiotic factor of the ecosystem that did not directly affect the fish. Could the fish population still be affected? How?

3. Give two factors that keep most populations in creation from experiencing a population explosion.

4. A species of lobster inhabits the crevices beneath a fringing coral-reef ecosystem. There are few openings under the corals, and every nook seems to be filled with a lobster. Is this struggle for living space an example of intraspecific or interspecific competition?

5. If a company is considering mass-harvesting a natural population of a specific organism, why is it important to know the organism's feeding habits as well as its predators?

6. a. The dinoflagellates called zooxanthellae are in a symbiotic relationship with coral. What type of symbiosis is this?

b. Cleaner fishes set up stations in the ocean, where they will feed on parasites and dead tissue of other fishes. What type of symbiosis is this?

c. What is the difference between these two examples of symbiosis?

7. Name the trophic levels in the following food chain: kelp, sea urchins, sea otters. In an ecological pyramid, which level has the most energy and largest population?

8. Is detritus a completely nonliving material?

9. Explain why knowing the primary productivity within an ecosystem does not help a scientist to guess the population of phytoplankton in that system.

10. What is the one important difference between the carbon cycle and the nitrogen cycle?

11. Describe the difference between a benthic organism and a pelagic organism.

12. Where is the aphotic zone in the ocean?

13. A benthic organism never sees sunlight, but it lives on the continental shelf. In what region of the ocean does it live?

14. In an aquarium, if there are not enough of a certain type of bacteria, the wastes from the fish cause a rise in the ammonia levels in the tank, which can harm the fish. In our discussion of the nitrogen cycle, what did we call the process by which these bacteria get rid of the ammonia?

15. In the carbon cycle, what gets rid of dissolved carbon dioxide in the ecosystem?

TEST FOR MODULE #9

1. Define the following terms:

a. Intertidal zone
b. Sessile
c. Desiccated
d. Vertical zonation
e. Ecological succession

2. What are the two major types of substrates in the intertidal zone?

3. Name one difficulty and one benefit of wave action for creatures living in the intertidal zone.

4. Name a strategy that a non-sessile intertidal organism must employ during high tide in order to avoid being thrashed about by the waves.

5. If a sessile organism cannot endure desiccation, how does it avoid desiccation in the upper intertidal area during low tide?

6. On a clear summer day, how will the temperature and salinity change in a tide pool during low tide?

7. Explain why a wave will bend, or refract, toward the shore if it approaches the shore at an angle.

8. If a beach has a canyon or sand bar offshore, will it have weak or strong wave action?

9. Why is space such an important factor to organisms in the intertidal?

10. Would salinity and temperature affect the upper or lower limits of living space for an intertidal organism?

11. In two different intertidal locations, a scientist finds bands of mussels. He notices that one location has sea stars present, while the other does not. In which location would you expect the band of mussels to be wider?

12. Once an intertidal area has reached a climax community, does this mean that no other organisms can ever move in? Why or why not?

13. Which zone of the rocky intertidal has the greatest diversity of organisms – the upper, middle, or lower intertidal?

14. What is the limiting resource of each of the three intertidal zones?

15. Which type of sediment allows water to move through more slowly – sand or mud? Why?

16. Why is zonation not noticeable in the muddy intertidal?

TEST FOR MODULE #10

1. Define the following terms:

a. Estuary   e. Wetlands
b. Euryhaline   f. Mudflats
c. Stenohaline   g. Meiofauna
d. Brackish   h. Channels

2. What caused the ocean levels of the world to rise enough to form most of the world's estuaries?

3. What is the most common substrate of an estuary? Why?

4. Why does an estuary have fluctuating salinity levels?

5. The figure below is a side-on view of a hypothetical estuary. Starting at the three X's in the figure, draw lines that delineate the salinity levels marked in the figure.

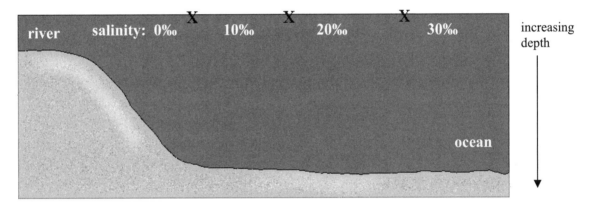

6. A scientist is studying an estuary in the Southern Hemisphere. If he is floating on a boat in the ocean and looking toward the shore, which side of the river will have the lowest salinity near the ocean?

7. A species of clam is found only in a narrow area of the center of an estuary. Is it most likely euryhaline, stenohaline, or a brackish species? Why?

8. Are salt marshes found in temperate or tropical climates?

9. What do the pneumatophores of black mangroves provide for the plants?

10. You are lost in a mangrove forest. If you are surrounded by white mangrove trees, are you at a relatively low, medium, or high elevation?

11. Why do some types of bacteria do well in the mudflats?

12. Explain why there are very few macroscopic species living on the surface of mudflats.

13. What is the relationship between the length of shorebirds' bills and the buried depths of estuarine organisms?

14. Why are channels ideal as nurseries for fishes?

15. As a rule, do estuaries provide less, just enough, or more organic material than needed for the organisms living there? If they do not provide enough, where do they get the rest, and if they provide too much, where does the excess go?

TEST FOR MODULE #11

1. Define the following terms:

a. Corallite   d. Fringing reef
b. Septa   e. Barrier reef
c. Columella   f. Atoll

2. If corals require shallow water in the warm tropics in order to grow, why are tropical areas such as the west coast of South America without reefs?

3. Explain how encrusting coralline algae aid in reef building.

4. Name a way that a coral can asexually reproduce and sexually reproduce to form another head of coral that is *not* connected to the parent coral.

5. A marine biologist is studying a coral reef that contains a large amount of branching coral. In which direction do the coral polyps mostly reproduce in order to create a branching form? In which direction do encrusting and boulder corals primarily reproduce?

6. Name one use of mucus for coral polyps.

7. Of the three regions within a fringing reef (reef flat, reef crest, and reef slope), which is the most seaward? Which is the most prolific location for coral?

8. What do scientists believe causes the "spur and groove" formations on a barrier reef?

9. What is the probable order of reef types that would form around a new oceanic volcanic island?

10. What is the name for the side of an atoll that receives the most wind and wave action?

11. Once established, a coral-reef ecosystem is nearly a self-sustaining ecosystem, requiring little outside nutrients in order to survive. Explain why.

12. What are the two major primary producers in a coral reef environment?

13. A coral reef has recently become overgrown by seaweeds. Name at least one possible reason this could have happened.

14. Name one way that a coral can attack a neighboring coral to obtain more living space.

15. The coral-reef ecosystem is a very productive as well as efficient ecosystem. How is the symbiotic relationship of mutualism a means of efficiency?

TEST FOR MODULE #12

1. Define the following terms:

a. Benthos
b. Nekton
c. Plankton

2. Would you find larger or smaller sediment particle sizes in turbulent waters? Why?

3. Where are these organisms located among the benthos: infauna, epifauna, and meiofauna?

4. What are at least two differences between the muddy-bottom soft-shelf community and the sandy-bottom soft-shelf community?

5. Detritus is the main food source in a soft-bottom shelf community. Is it vegetated or unvegetated?

6. A teacher shows you just the bottom of a green marine organism. It has roots. Is it an alga or a seagrass?

7. Since few organisms feed directly on seagrasses, how does the community take advantage of all the food they provide?

8. A shelf community has very little infauna. Do algae or seagrasses most likely grow there?

9. Name two ways that algae can defend themselves from grazers.

10. A shelf community is cold and hard-bottomed. It has a lot of sediment constantly floating in it. Would you expect to find kelp to be plentiful here?

11. Why is the third dimension of a canopy important to kelp forest organisms?

12. You see a lot of dead, floating giant kelp washing up on shore. What is the most likely explanation for this?

13. A single cell from a giant kelp has two chromosomes for each pair. Would you expect the adult from which this cell came to be large or small?

TEST FOR MODULE #13

1. Define the following terms:

a. Epipelagic zone
b. Meroplankton
c. Neuston
d. Vertical migration

e. Dissolved organic matter (DOM)
f. Microbial loop
g. Upwelling

2. Does most human activity occur in the neritic or oceanic zone of the epipelagic?

3. Distinguish between holoplankton and meroplankton.

4. Why are picoplankton important for the cycling of nutrients in the epipelagic?

5. A marine biologist does a plankton tow in the epipelagic and collects many species of zooplankton. Which organisms will most likely be the largest group collected?

6. Larvaceans are important predators in the epipelagic as well as providing an important food supply for other species. Explain their special role in the food web.

7. Most nektonic species are carnivorous predators. Give an example of a large nektonic organism that is not a carnivorous predator.

8. An epipelagic organism has many feathery projections on its body. Is it most likely planktonic or nektonic? Why?

9. Explain the benefit of swim bladders and dark, myoglobin-rich interior muscles in nektonic species such as tuna.

10. The violet shell (*Janthina*) is a predator that suspends itself upside down at the surface of the water using air-filled bubbles. Upon which group of organisms (plankton, nekton, or neuston) does this creature feed?

11. Why are most epipelagic nekton silver and blue in color?

12. Which epipelagic creatures undergo vertical migration?

13. The microbial loop is sometimes referred to as a food web within a food web. Explain why this might be so.

14. The equator has a relatively high amount of primary productivity, yet just north and south of it, productivity greatly is diminished. Explain why it is so high at the equator.

15. How is the weather in India connected to the weather in Peru and Chile?

TEST FOR MODULE #14

1. Define the following terms:

a. Mesopelagic zone   d. Bioluminescence
b. Photophores   e. Chemosynthesis
c. Hydrothermal vent

2. As depth increases in the ocean, the abundance of life and the quantity of food decrease. Explain why this is so.

3. Suppose you drop a thermometer into the ocean and monitor its temperature reading as it sinks. You suddenly notice a sharp drop in the temperature. In which zone of the ocean is the thermometer?

4. Suppose the thermometer in the question above has a pressure-sensitive device as well. Suppose you continue to watch both the pressure and the temperature as the devices continue to sink. Assuming you already saw the sharp drop in temperature mentioned in the previous problem, which would you expect to change more drastically after that point: pressure or temperature?

5. How do mesopelagic fishes compare in size to their epipelagic counterparts?

6. Why do most mesopelagic fishes have a broad diet?

7. What physical features are typically possessed by mesopelagic fish that find their food through vertical migration?

8. How are ventrally located photophores helpful in camouflage?

9. What physical feature differentiates the deep sea from the mesopelagic?

10. What two chemicals must an organism produce in order to perform bioluminescence? What does each chemical do?

11. As compared to an organism's ability to get food in the deep sea water column, how difficult is it for a deep sea floor individual to find food?

12. The figure below shows a food web for the deep sea floor. Fill in the blanks labeled a-c.

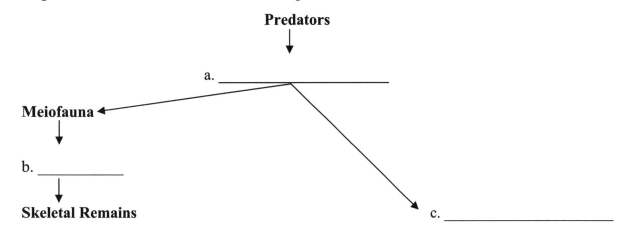

13. A marine biologist studied a sunken whale carcass at a specific location on the deep sea floor along with the organisms living on it. Just two years later, scientists returned to the same location to discover bare ocean floor. What happened to this community?

TEST FOR MODULE #15

1. Define the following terms:

a. Clupeoid fishes   c. Sustainable yield
b. Gadoid fishes   d. Mariculture

2. What is the fisheries' term used for fish that are harvested for food?

3. How does coastal upwelling enhance fish populations?

4. Which group of fishes are most often caught by purse seines?

5. Which group of fishes are most often caught by trawls?

6. In the 1950s, the Peruvian anchoveta, a clupeoid fish like the anchovy, was heavily fished for use as fish meal and oil. Anchovetas were heavily fished until the early 1970s when stocks were suddenly severely decreased, and the anchoveta fishing industry collapsed. What was the most likely cause of the decrease in anchoveta stocks?

7. Name two ways fisheries can aid overfished populations in recovering without completely halting fishing altogether.

8. Which type of mariculture involves controlling the water quality?

9. Explain why it would be difficult to raise tunas in a mariculture facility.

10. What does the term "renewable resource" mean? Give an example of a renewable marine resource.

11. What are the benefits that reverse osmosis has over distillation in desalinization?

12. In a few areas of the world, such as in Norway, there are curious-looking structures similar to windmills that are located under water. For what are they used?

TEST FOR MODULE #16

1. Define the following terms:

    a. Eutrophication   c. Biomagnification
    b. Nonbiodegradable   d. Fouling organisms

2. Differentiate the following activities as indirectly or directly affecting an estuary:

    a. Dredging the bottom to allow larger ships access
    b. Fertilizer runoff from a farm 25 miles inland
    c. Filling in parts of the estuary with sand to support oceanfront property
    d. Trawling for shrimp
    e. Diverting river water upstream to supply fresh water for crops

3. A tropical fish dealer receives a shipment of marine fish, 90% of which die after the first week. It turns out that the collectors used cyanide to capture the fish. Besides this direct effect on the fish, what would be an indirect effect to the coral reef of the use of poison in the water?

4. Why is chlorine not the best solution for treating sewage to be dumped into the ocean?

5. Explain the following statement: Marshes are secondary purifying plants for raw sewage.

6. An ecosystem is exposed to a large oil spill, but it recovers from the exposure fairly quickly. What can you say about the wave action in this ecosystem?

7. Suppose you are looking at two difference ecosystems: an estuary and a deep-ocean seafloor. You find oil in both. Most likely, which ecosystem's oil is the result of natural processes?

8. You are looking at how two pollutants affect a marine ecosystem. Both are fat-soluble chemicals, but one is biodegradable and one is not. As you compare planktivorous fish to marine mammals in the ecosystem, which chemical will you expect to find larger quantities of in the marine mammals?

9. Chlorinated hydrocarbons are subject to biomagnification. Name another type of chemical also subject to biomagnification.

10. What type of pollutant can kill or harm *any* marine organism without being eaten?

11. How can Styrofoam® be dangerous for marine life?

12. A demolition company suggests cleaning the rubble from several buildings it has destroyed and dumping it in a shallow, sandy-bottomed area of the ocean. Although some are against this proposal, the local marine biologists are quite supportive of it. Why?